Victoria,

# ARISE
*Finding Healing through Broken Pieces*

## SHAMEKA DANIELS

Published by Godzchild Publications
a division of Godzchild, Inc.
22 Halleck St., Newark, NJ 07104
www.godzchildproductions.net

Printed in the United States of America 2018 - 1st Edition

Library of Congress Cataloging-in-Publications Data
ARISE/Shameka Daniels

ISBN 978-1727188066

1. Shameka 2. Daniels

2018

## DEDICATION

*To the three most important people in my life who have
my whole heart, Dharius, Seth & Gabe. You have been
my inspiration to work through my brokenness and find
wholeness. It is my prayer that I am to you everything I was
created to be.*

*To anyone who has lived life feeling empty, discouraged, hurt,
unloved, lost, or broken...I understand. God has given me the
courage and confidence to share a part of me so that you can
find your wholeness, too. I love you and God loves you too.*

# TABLE OF Contents

# FOREWORD

There are a number of different words that can be used to describe what you are about to read —*genuine, transparent, encouraging, inspirational* — and although all of these words are appropriate, there is one word (in my mind) that sticks out head-and-shoulders above the rest. This word can only be used by someone like me because I have a unique relationship with the author that no one else has; and that word is credible.

*Arise* is a credible testimonial and an inspirational, life-giving document. I say that because my wife has literally practiced everything that she preaches in this book. For more than 20 years, I have had a front row seat in my wife's transformative journey. I have witnessed and been blessed by the tremendous growth, spiritual awareness, and inimitable wisdom that has come from her experiences. I have watched her pray, cry, stretch herself, and grow, as she aims to live her life, in passionate pursuit, to become the woman she is called to be.

I have witnessed her evolve from broken to whole, from timid to assertive, from apprehensive to confident, from weak to strong—and I have been inspired by her journey to become a man worthy of a woman like this.

It has been said that God uses our stories for his glory; and I have never been more confident in the accuracy of that axiom, than I am right now. This book is catalytic and compassionate. This book is personal and impactful. As an observer of the awesome work that God has done in my wife's life, I am convinced now more than ever, that God will give us beauty for ashes, turn our mourning into dancing, and give us the garment of praise for the spirit of heaviness.

As I celebrate what God has done in the past and as we benefit from the lessons learned in the present, I am filled with anticipation of what God will continue to do in the future; and I am excited about the ways God will use this book to change the lives of others around the world.

Today, I stand on the sidelines as a proud husband, and I am honored to passionately proclaim to my amazing wife and to women like her...LIONESS ARISE!!!

-Dharius Daniels

# ACKNOWLEDGMENTS

Writing a book like this isn't easy because I have opened my life for others to see. I want to thank my husband, Dharius Daniels, for encouraging me to write about my journey, for supporting and loving me when it wasn't always easy, and for believing in me. I love you and I would not be the woman I am today, if it wasn't for you. You 'next leveled' me. You are my definition of a knight in shining armor.

To my boys, Seth & Gabe, thank you for being my biggest fans. You boys make being a mom easy.

To my parents, Robert & Eleanor, thank you for always pushing me to be the best girl I can be. You have been supportive in everything I have done and I appreciate you.

To my girls, Patrice, Phaedra, and Rhonda, thank you for your presence and encouragement.

To Shaun Saunders, thank you for helping me to make sense out of my words. I hope this book will change the lives of others.

To Dr. R.A. & Victory Vernon, thank you for igniting a fire in me that pushed me to be a better wife, mother and woman. Thank you for your truthfulness, your love and your encouragement. I'm grateful that you are in my life.

To Denise Boggs, thank you for being a lifeguard. You have mothered and nurtured me to a place of wholeness. My heart can now give and receive love. I will forever be grateful to you for your love, prayers, encouragement and dedication to me.

To Jacob & Michelle Aranza, thank you for seeing a diamond in the rough. Your invitation to the Arise Conference confirmed that it was time for me to step out and be courageous. Thank you for believing in me.

To my church family, you have seen me transform into the Lioness God has created me to be. Thank you for loving and supporting me. Thank you for being a church that receives and helps to change the world.

Finally, I want to thank God for healing me and for filling me with an overflow of hope, joy, and peace.

# INTRODUCTION

Imagine growing up as a little girl who had everything she wanted, but feeling like something was missing. Imagine hearing comments like "you must have been a mistake." You might guess that this girl feels lonely and rejected.

Imagine that same girl excited to go to school in the hopes that she would find acceptance. But instead of getting what she hoped for, she is constantly teased and bullied for things about herself that she cannot change. You might guess that this girl feels unworthy. There is nothing she can do to get the love she so desperately searches for.

Imagine that girl needing someone to talk to. She confides in family members and friends, but they tell her secrets to strangers and crush her trust. You might guess that this girl is untrusting of everyone, so she put up walls to protect herself.

See this girl, adjusting everything about herself just to fit in. She changes her appearance. She changes her interests. She stops hanging out with positive influences and starts hanging out with people who take her focus away from the things that really matter.

Imagine that girl struggling with isolation all of her life, and then finally finding someone who accepts her for who she is; only for that someone to drown in a pool unexpectedly. You might guess that this girl is devastated. She's heartbroken. Everyone who accepts her is taken away from her. Everyone who rejects her is brought close.

See this girl searching. She's searching to fill her emptiness. She's searching for someone to fill that void. She's looking for attention. Imagine that girl spiraling down that staircase of esteem more and more.

The older she gets, the older the pain gets. It grows from bad to worse. She just wants to be loved. So, she puts her energy into relationships that are a waste of time, friendships that take advantage of her, and opportunities that are not fulfilling.

She's in her 30's now, and something is still missing. She's married now, and something is still missing. She's a mother now, and something is still missing. She's been trying to work her way out of this void, love her way out of this void, give her way out of this void, but then it dawns on her: that her calling is not her healing. It dawns on her that she has been wearing a mask for decades, and it's just too heavy to do on her own. She needs to make a change. But how? When? Who do I talk to? What do I read? Imagine this girl writing a book for you to see how she did it.

This is my story…and this was my struggle…but then, I decided to ARISE.

# CHAPTER 1

# ARISE FROM REJECTION

*Is anyone crying for help? God is listening, ready to rescue you. If your heart is broken, you'll find God right there; if you're kicked in the gut, he'll help you catch your breath. Disciples so often get into trouble; still, God is there every time. He's your bodyguard, shielding every bone; not even a finger gets broken.*

–Psalms 34:17-20 MSG

For as long as I can remember, I have always wanted to fit in. As a child, I longed for companionship. As a teen, I looked for connection. As a young adult, I searched for acceptance. I gravitated toward the "cool kids"—you know, the people who were popular, witty, and charming. I wanted to be a part of the "it crowd," but these "it people" never really wanted to be around me. So I did everything I could do to win their approval. If I had to change my hair, I did it. If I had to break the rules, I did it. I tried my best to gain their affirmation, and every time I went beyond the border of my limits to do something to impress someone in the "crowd", I would encounter the one thing I tried my best to avoid: *rejection*. Rejection was

*Rejection was like waking up to acne on the day of the prom.*

the friend I never asked for. Rejection was the burden I didn't want to bear. She was a thorn in my flesh. She showed up to parties that I didn't invite her to attend. Who knows where it came from, or why the pain of it has crippled me so many times in my past. I'm sure it had something to do with my childhood. Doesn't everything have something to do with your childhood?

I grew up as an only child in a home that always felt so cold; so empty; so colorless. My mother and father loved me, and they loved God, but I didn't have anyone in my home that I could relate to. I had siblings but John was 18 when I was born and Ronnie was 24 and married with a son of his own before I learned how to crawl. I didn't make much noise as a child, but I was crying for help. I was searching for someone to see me. I needed to know that I was celebrated and not just tolerated. I needed to know that I was seen and not just heard. I always wanted a sister close to my age. In my mind, she would talk to me, play with me, and keep me company. But because I didn't receive the kind of attention I longed for, I tried to create it in people, places and things that were not healthy for me.

It began in middle school. Like most tweens, the highlight of my entire middle school experience was cafeteria time. During lunch, everybody would run to their posse, clan, or clique, and they would talk sports, fashion, or homework. Well, in my school, the same was true. Everybody had a clique, but there was a group that I really wanted to hang out with. Problem is, they loved to make fun of me. Constantly and incessantly, they would pick on me about things that I couldn't change—things about my physical characteristics that I didn't ask for, and things about me that I didn't see as a major issue, but the more they laughed, the more I began to see myself as a joke. They talked about me in front of me, and they made fun of me loud enough that others around the table would chime in and add their harmful comments as well. You would think that I would get up from the table, walk away from the group and find another group to hang with, right? Wrong. Instead, I stayed at the table. I stayed at the place that made me feel small. I stayed in a room that didn't value my contribution. I taught myself, right in middle school, how to settle. I taught myself that I had to accept whatever people did to me, in order to gain their acceptance of me. In the presence of my enemies, I let them laugh at me. I didn't stop it. I entertained it. I encouraged it. I accepted their harsh words as common cafeteria talk. Even though the group wasn't good for me, I stayed in a place I should've left because I didn't know how to walk away.

By the end of my middle school years, my relationship with rejection became the norm. In Mississippi, social groups were a big part of our academic identity. Everyone belonged to something. Everyone participated in a social club or a sports team, and the Pink Panthers were the happening group in middle school that every girl wanted to be a part of. But in order to be a Pink Panther, you had to embody the Pink Panther spirit. Pink Panther's looked a certain way. They spoke a certain way. They wore their hair a certain way, and they only hung out with a certain "kind of person" at certain, elite times. I wanted so badly to be a Pink Panther. The group at the cafeteria table didn't want me, so eventually I just looked for someone else to accept me. I was willing to do whatever I needed to do, to join the group. But one of the Pink Panther girls didn't like the texture of my hair or the color of my skin. There were very few black girls where I went to school, so she told everybody that it was my hair, she didn't like, but I knew the truth. She told me that my look didn't match their look, so they wouldn't let me join. They just told me I wasn't fit to be in their group, and once again, I was rejected… for something as minor as "skin color" and "hair." No big deal, right? Just find another group to be a part of right? Wrong. I folded to the pressure. I hid in my cave and internalized everything they said. I started looking at my hair and asking my mother to change it. Nobody else knew it but I did. I started criticizing the beautiful parts of me that made me unique, and instead of building myself up, I tore my own self down. I know. I know. I know I should've been able to lean on my Christian values. I should've been able to start my own group. I should've been able to praise my way through it. But each time I experienced rejection, I lost another part of Shameka.

Not before long, I was doing anything and everything to fit in. Studies show that when a person struggles with acceptance, there comes a point where they will do anything to get it. So if they were a nerd in school, they will become the rebel. If they were organized at home, they will clutter every part of their home. In short, people who want acceptance will swing from one extreme to the other. That was me to the tee. I had always been a hard-working student. I turned in my work on time. I sat in the front of the class. I participated. I even helped friends with their homework. But I noticed that a few of the rebels would come together to plan days like "National Skip Day." On one particular day, everyone in school agreed to skip school, and while this was totally opposite from how I was raised, I signed up to be one of the first people to skip school on National Skip Day. The more rebellious I became, the more everyone seemed to like me, so I did whatever I had to do to keep others close to me. I would go wherever my "friends" wanted me to go. I would agree to do unbelievable things like go to Pizza Hut on skip day and leave the restaurant without paying. Now, my momma raised me to do right by people. She raised me to be a respectful young girl, and I knew it was wrong to leave a restaurant without paying, but I needed to fit in so badly, that I was willing to compromise my standards for company. This day, however, I couldn't go through with the plan entirely, so when everyone got up to leave the restaurant, I told them that I needed to use the restroom. When I returned inside of the Pizza Hut, I paid the bill and left without anyone knowing. Everyone else thought I was "down for the cause," but I knew the truth. I just wanted someone to see me.

Have you ever wanted to be seen? Not just from the outside but from the inside? Have you ever wanted someone to hear you crying even when you were saying no words? Have you ever walked around in a room and felt completely invisible? Like most young girls, I wanted someone to accept me. All of me. I didn't ask to be different but even my good differences, seemed to be unappealing to the people I wanted to be around. My mother raised me to take my education seriously. "Do your best and reach for the stars" was the constant mantra we heard in our home. As a result, I did my best. I applied myself in school and I did very well in high school; so much so, I was offered the opportunity to graduate a year earlier than others in my class. The one catch was that I needed to enroll in summer school to take a class that wasn't offered during my third year of high school. The summer program I enrolled in, was typically for people in Jackson who took that particular class and failed, so they

*Rejection becomes present whenever acceptance is absent.*

were coming to summer school to retake the class again. Imagine how uncomfortable it was when I introduced myself in summer school as the girl who was only there so I could graduate early. Immediately, a group of three girls decided they were going to turn my summer school experience into a living nightmare. Every day, they bullied me. Every day, they snarled at me. They wouldn't let one day go by without saying something or doing something negative. But the day they threatened to fight me, I had had enough. I told my mother I wasn't going back to summer school; instead, I was going to quit. My mother wouldn't allow me to do it, and my cousin somehow intervened and handled those girls without me knowing, but I almost gave up on graduating early, all because I didn't want to constantly subject myself to this cycle of rejection.

How many things have you stopped doing so you could avoid the possibility of rejection? How many dreams did you bury because people around you were too intimidated by you to congratulate you? In the end, I graduated early, but I still couldn't go on the senior trip and do the things that other seniors did to commemorate their graduation. By this point though, it didn't really matter. I just wanted out. I needed to get out of the high school bubble. And I had convinced myself that if I could just get out of high school, relief would be on the other side of graduation. I just knew that when I got to college, my rejection issues would be over. I wouldn't be forced to do anything I didn't want to do, and people would learn to love me for who I am or leave me alone. But the cycle continued. Different people. Different scenarios. Same issue.

They used to say in the South "every round goes higher and higher," and I couldn't agree more. In college, I went out to pledge for a sorority. I thought the Pink Panthers were bad. But the girls in the sorority were vicious with a vengeance. Like usual, I slipped right back into old habits of cooking dinner for everyone, paying for someone's food, staying up all night to help my "sisters" with their college work or their webpages, but nothing I could do for them stopped them from sabotaging my pledging experience. A few of the girls decided that they would get me kicked out of the pledging process, and when I realized what was happening I was devastated. Being in this sorority had always been a dream of mine. It was something my aunt encouraged me to do. My entire family saw it as a major mark in the life of a young woman (it was a family tradition). Thankfully, the tables turned and someone else on our line exposed the truth, but I almost lost out on a major personal accomplishment all because someone didn't want me to be a part. I was grateful that I crossed, but I couldn't stop thinking about how many opportunities would've been taken from me all because someone had rejected me—for things about me that I couldn't control. When I think about my story, I know I'm not alone. I know I'm not the only woman who has downplayed her contribution for acceptance from the wrong crowd. I can't be the only one who has allowed rejection to define me. To those who can relate, I want to ask you: how long will rejection keep defining you? I was crying for

> *How long will other people's words and actions keep imprisoning you?*

help. I was longing for God. But I didn't know how to rise from the residue of rejection, so I started looking for positions or opportunities to give me value. And when I got rejected from an internship opportunity that I applied for, that was the final straw! I had had enough. Even though I ended up getting the job, I still wanted to know why I wasn't enough to be someone's first pick? Why did the kids at the table make fun of me in middle school? Why did the Pink Panthers not like my hair? Why did the girls in summer school want to fight me? Why did the sorority girls plot to get me kicked off the line? I was spiraling into an unending sea of questions, and these questions followed me into adulthood. For decades, I didn't know how to get myself out of this trap, until I realized that I had to rise.

## RISE UP!

*Is anyone crying for help? God is listening, ready to rescue you. If your heart is broken, you'll find God right there; if you're kicked in the gut, he'll help you catch your breath.*

*Disciples so often get into trouble; still, God is there every time. He's your bodyguard, shielding every bone; not even a finger gets broken.*

–Psalms 34:17-20 MSG

My rising moment happened when I truly decided to turn to God to rescue me, instead of looking for others to do it for me. I had to get to the root of this rejection issue because I was blaming people for things they said, but I wasn't aware of what was underneath all of this pain. Underneath my rejection issues was a need to belong; a need to be seen and a need to be heard. In order for you to rise from the scars of rejection, the first thing I want you to do is ACKNOWLEDGE where you are and what you need. When we acknowledge where we are, we are not afraid to take off the blinders and tell the hard truth to ourselves. I had to tell the hard truth to myself even though it wasn't a truth I was proud of. I, Shameka Daniels, had consistently compromised my values to gain approval from others. That was the truth. I, Shameka Daniels, had lost my center because I was holding on to people who weren't holding on to me. That was the truth. The other truth was that I was looking for people in my present to fulfill a void that should've been fulfilled in my past. That was the truth, and there was an underlying pattern in my life that I didn't want to see for myself.

Now, I don't blame my family for what I experienced. A part of this healing journey has taught me to own my mistakes, and not to project my process onto anyone. So, I take ownership for every decision I made; and at the same time, as you will come to discover in this book, everything has a root. Every decision is like a tree. The world sees the branches, but you know the root. Your spouse sees the branches of your actions, but you know the root. And if the root is not connected to its source, then a tree cannot produce fruit. If the roots are damaged, then the growth of the tree will be stunted. As we begin to look at each issue in this book, it is not just important to acknowledge the truth and take off the blinders. But secondly, it is important that we UNCOVER the hidden things, and identify the root. Luke 8:17 says "for nothing is secret that shall not be made manifest; neither anything hidden that shall not be known and come to light." Take a moment and answer these questions. What is beneath your need to please? What is underneath your perfectionism? Why do you feel the need to over-talk sometimes? Or why do you choose not to speak at all? Everything has a root. The root of my rejection was loneliness. Once I uncovered the root, I was then able to REPLACE the lie. The lie I told myself was that nobody cared, and only people could make me feel whole. The longer I believed the lie, the longer I turned to people to make me whole. But when people disappointed me, let me down or rejected me, I would fall into a deeper state of loneliness, and I would have to search for more people to fill a problem they didn't create. Do you see how

*As long as we turn to people instead of God, we will always be disappointed.*

rejection traps you? But one day, I not only acknowledged the pain, uncovered the truth, and replaced the lie. I then started to EXAMINE the side-effects of rejection. Examination helps you to count up the cost. Examination helps you to assess the reality of a situation. And the truth is, rejection has side-effects. The more life I gave to rejection, the more death I experienced in my soul. The side-effects of rejection are mistrust, abandonment, fear, and resentment. I couldn't trust anyone new to come into my life because I thought they would use me. And once they used me, they would leave me so I felt abandoned. I began to fear new friendships. If one person hurt me, I would resent them forever. The side-effects were worse than the rejection itself, and I decided to rise because my pain was too expensive to manage without God.

After you ACKNOWLEDGE, UNCOVER, and EXAMINE, then you need to ARISE and make the change. Making the change looks different for all of us, but the first thing we all can do is turn to God instead of turning to people. When we turn to God we are confiding in the one who will never hurt us, who will never leave us, and who will never forsake us. I accepted the truth of the verse we read at the beginning of this chapter—God is there every time. God is there with us when we feel alone. God is there with us when we feel helpless. God is there with us when we feel unusable. When I made the change, I did some small things in my life that made a huge difference. I turned to God in prayer before I vented to my friends. I made my time with God my priority instead of my last resort. I also learned how to build my devotional life with him, and to work at my own pace—and let me tell you! God began to minister to the pain of rejection. God began to replace the lie of my feelings with the truth of my faith. As I turned to God, He helped me to remove the façade. He also helped me to repair broken relationships. He healed the broken parts of me so that I could identify the brokenness in others.

When you finally rise from rejection, you will gain the power to examine who you have hurt and build a bridge to reconcile with the people you damaged while you were damaged. Most importantly, you can embrace the ongoing healing process of God's love and grace. I had to learn not to beat myself up so much, but accept the season that I was in, and to trust that God would get me to the place I needed to be, when I needed to be there. The same is true for you. Don't beat yourself up. Take this journey one day at a time, one step at a time. If God can do that for me, then I am certain that God can do the same for you! It's time to RISE UP!

# RISE UP!

1. Acknowledge: take off the blinders

2. Uncover: identify the root – replace the lie.

3. Examine: evaluate the side-effects of rejection

4. Arise: Make the Change

You were created by God and in His eyes, you are fearfully and wonderfully made.
You are good enough and you are accepted by Him.

*"For you formed my inward parts; you knitted me together in my mother's womb. I praise you, for I am fearfully and wonderfully made. Wonderful are your works; my soul knows it very well." Psalm 139:13 ESV*

You can rejoice because God will pour into you at your emptiest state. Have faith in Him and He will give you the strength and endurance as He builds you up.

*"Through him we have also obtained access by faith into this grace in which we stand, and we rejoice in hope of the glory of God. Not only that, but we rejoice in our sufferings, knowing that suffering produces endurance, and endurance produces character, and character produces hope, and hope does not put us to shame, because God's love has been poured into our hearts through the Holy Spirit who has been given to us." Romans 5-5:2 ESV*

## PRAYER

God, you created me perfect in your eyes. Help me to see in me what you see. I have experienced rejection, and it has caused some emptiness in me. God I'm asking you to fill that voided place, and today I'm releasing the need to have someone or something to fill it. God help me to take the blinders off and see how rejection has controlled me. Help me to be honest with myself and to discover the root of my rejection. I need healing from the pain that I have felt and strength to address the side effects that have been a result of it. God, I desire wholeness in this area and I am committed to arise. I will make the necessary changes to find my wholeness. Amen.

## CHAPTER 2

# ARISE FROM INSECURITY

*Your hands have made and fashioned me; give me understanding that I may learn your commandments.*

—Psalms 119:73 -(ESV)

How do you rise from insecurity when everyone believes in you...except you? We are living in an amazing time. Technology has advanced. Women are leading in ways they never have before. The world is literally at our fingertips. And at the same time, more and more people admit they have never felt so insecure about life. I can't tell you how many women have confided in me about their insecurities over the last few years. A lot of us are doing well for ourselves. We have degrees, we have financial stability, and we have a plan A, B, and C. But we are insecure about whether or not we can walk into everything God has for us.

*Am I enough?*
*What if I fail?*
*Who will show up?*
*What if I never get what I want?*
*Why not choose someone else?*

These are just a few of the questions we ask ourselves, not because we are incompetent, but because we are insecure.

*Insecurity is uncertainty or anxiety about oneself. It is birthed from the lie that you are not enough.*

Insecure people always seek validation from others. Insecure people tend to be self-conscious and very critical of themselves. We are apprehensive about most things and fearful of just about everything. If someone is insecure, they lack confidence. They tend to focus on the negative instead of the positive. Instead of embracing every opportunity with joy, insecure people approach most situations by asking the question, "What is wrong with me?"

That was me.

My issues as a child reinforced my insecurities as a woman. My insecurities were like weeds. If you don't kill weeds at the root, then they will continue to grow back. That's what happened all throughout my life. If someone pushed me away or excluded me, I automatically assumed the problem was me. *Shameka is too skinny. Shameka is too tall. Shameka is too this. Shameka is too that.* Whatever the critique was, it all boiled down to one conclusion: I wasn't enough. I didn't realize how harmful this mindset was until I started to see how unaddressed insecurities can impair your perspective about everything.

When I grew up, I had an image of the perfect family. It was based on the television shows I watched. I loved *The Brady Bunch* and *Family Matters*. I thought everyone's family was supposed to look like that. In my mind, every family consisted of a two-parent home, a warm and loving mother, a cool and supportive father, encouraging siblings, a playful environment, and a wonderfully wholesome life. I imagined that every family sat down at the dinner table together and talked about their day. Every girl learned how to put on makeup from her mom. Every boy learned how to put on a tie from his dad.

Family equaled quality time. It was about spending time together. That included holiday parties with brothers and sisters; hanging out with aunts and uncles; eating on Sunday's with extended family members. But my experience was different than that. My brothers were grown men when I was born. I felt lonely a lot and desired to have that "TV family connection." I wanted a sister more than anything. I wanted to play dress-up and tag with my siblings. This deficit caused more loneliness, especially because I grew up closer to one side of my family than the other. This left me asking all kinds of questions. In the end, I told myself that I must be the problem.

Maybe your family dynamic is different than mine but have you ever assumed the problem was you, growing up? Have you ever thought to yourself...*maybe something is wrong with me. Maybe joy left in my family when I was born.* Have you ever wrestled with guilt because you felt like an inconvenience? I knew my parents were happy that I arrived but I always felt out of place. I always pointed to myself as the problem…not because my parents made me feel that way, but because random people would see the age difference between me and my brothers, and assume I was the "oops" baby. In their mind, I was the burden. I was the issue. Eventually, I began to internalize that. *Maybe they were right. Maybe I was the reason we couldn't be like what I saw on television.* As a result, I began to turn to outside relationships to give me inside validation.

All throughout high school, I dated guys who could build me up and validate me. I hung out with friends who made me feel like I was enough. It didn't matter if they were verbally abusive or manipulative, as long as they told me what I wanted to hear, I would give all of myself to them. I didn't really know how to stand up for myself. That concept was foreign to me. Over time, I taught myself to accept whatever I was given, and I overcompensated by giving myself to others even if they didn't give themselves to me.

*This pattern followed me into my college years, where I met a really cute guy named Dharius.*

The first time I laid eyes on him, he was at a social gathering in college with his friends. I was hanging out with my line sisters. He saw my line sister and sat next to her; I knew she had a boyfriend so I sat next to

Dharius to get his attention. That didn't work! I still didn't get his attention, instead of picking me, he picked my line sister to talk to. Minutes after meeting the man who would one day become my husband, insecurity started preaching that same old sermon: *Why didn't I get his attention? What did he see in her that he didn't see in you?* If you saw me at that event, you would've never known I was insecure. I was dressed to impress. My hair was laid. As the young girls might say in today's times, I was snatched! But it was all a cover up. Over time, I learned to protect myself by hiding behind false confidence. I masked my insecurity with nonchalance. I never let people see my brokenness. Even if it hurt me, I acted like it didn't bother me. I learned how to disguise my insecurity so well that people thought I was way more confident than I was. In Dharius's mind, I was the light-skinned conceited girl. But if he had known the truth, he would've discovered that I only believed I was pretty when other people told me so.

He didn't pick me that night. *Insert sad music.* But I picked him. I didn't ask him out directly because I was too afraid to be rejected. Instead, I chose the safe route. Before the event was over, I wrote my number on a piece of paper. I walked over to him as confidently as I could (I'm sure I was wearing the best pair of heels that I could find). I gave him the piece of paper and then whispered in his ear, "Call me if you're interested." My walk-away game was strong! I sashayed to the other side of the room as if I had to use the bathroom but I didn't have anywhere to go. I just stood there waiting to see if he would take the bait.

He took it. The next week, I got a phone call from him, and we spoke briefly. I thought it was a great conversation, but I guess my discernment was off. He disappeared for months. I literally did not hear from him for two or three months after that! *Are you kidding me?* Most girls would've looked in the mirror and said, "Girl, you are the gift. If he doesn't recognize your worth, walk away and find someone who does." But that wasn't me. Insecurity rushed back into the room and began preaching another sermon in my ear: *you see, he didn't want you in the first place. He only called you the first time because he felt bad. If a man is interested, he will be persistent about getting to know you. That man don't want you. Nobody wants you. You're not enough.*

Those were the lies insecurity told me and I believed it, until I found out the truth. Dharius had been calling me, but my roommate wouldn't relay the messages. Isn't it funny how the enemy will whisper lies in your ear? When Dharius and I finally spoke, he clarified what had happened, and one conversation corrected months of lies I had told myself. If you're reading this and you have ever struggled with insecurity, listen to me. Get all of the facts before you disqualify yourself.

> Don't let your mind take you where your life has not invited you.

Dharius and I began to talk on a regular basis. He was cool. He was very smart. I was definitely feeling him. We didn't rush into dating when I was in college. There were phases. First, you would "talk" to someone and get to know them. Then you would add a title to it (boyfriend/girlfriend). Then, you would start going out on dates. During our "talking phase," we spoke a lot over the phone. Dharius told me about his goals and career aspirations. The first thing he told me was that he was called to the ministry. He knew he wanted to be a lawyer but he also wanted to preach. By this point, he had already preached his first sermon and he was pretty confident that his life would land him in the church.

*That's nice,* I replied. But in my head I was thinking, "If this man thinks I am going to marry a preacher, he has another thing coming!" My mind was not thinking about full-time ministry at all! I wasn't that girl. I went to bible study on Tuesday and Wednesday. I went to "college events" on Thursday and Saturday, and then I went to

> I was a Christian, but I wasn't living like one every day of the week.

church on Sunday. I wasn't committed to the Lord like he was, so when he told me he was thinking about going into the ministry, I should've ended the conversation right there. Now all along, God was calling me but I wasn't listening. I remember going to a college bible study my freshman year, and a guy named Robert prophesied to me. He told me I was going to marry a preacher. I didn't receive that prophecy; I remember laughing and telling myself, "He missed God." My life didn't match that prophecy at all! I was totally fine with going to church and coming home, living my life, doing my work, and building my career. When Dharius told me he had ministry aspirations, Robert's words came back to my mind. I didn't say anything at the time.

I loved God and I wanted a relationship with Him, but I had some growing up to do (spiritually speaking). When we first began "talking," we were like oil and vinegar. I loved R&B and Hip-Hop; he loved Fred Hammond and Kirk Franklin. I was very blunt and I said whatever came to mind; he was more calculated and thoughtful of what he said and didn't say. So, we connected in the beginning, and then, the relationship drifted. During that time, his distance made me feel like something was wrong with me. *Here we go again—insecurity was causing me to question myself.* I figured we wouldn't speak again, and then one day, I saw him at a sorority event. Like clockwork, we started talking again. Eventually, he told me that he knew I was the one God made for him, and I felt the same way.

Our first date as boyfriend and girlfriend was not the movies. It wasn't a long walk in the park. Dharius decided to take me to a church crusade. The evangelist preaching was a popular megachurch pastor in the south and he was in town at the Jackson Coliseum. So Dharius drove to pick me up (we lived an hour away from each other), and we went to hear the evangelist preach. I was down for the cause, but I couldn't wrap my head around going to see a preacher for our first date. Nevertheless, I went and we learned even more about each other during that time. Dharius was sent into my life to "next level" me, but I was still listening to my R&B. One day, he took my CDs, threw them out, and the first Christian song I ever listened to, on repeat, was "Delivered" by Christopher Lewis. Then Dharius bought me "Pages of Life" by Fred Hammond. His goal was to introduce me to a better life, but my insecurities made me feel as if I wasn't good enough. I would always pay attention to his criticism of me. I never really focused on the positive outcome he was trying to introduce me to. Consider the pattern. Insecurity began when I was a child because I saw something on television that didn't match my reality. Then, I began to question myself in middle school, high school and college. The weeds of insecurity continued to grow higher and higher, and they didn't stop when I got married.

During our first years as husband and wife, Dharius was in seminary at Princeton. We had just relocated from Mississippi to New Jersey. As I said earlier, my husband is a brilliant man. He is articulate, calm, thoughtful, and poised. When he speaks, everyone pays attention. He was working on his master's degree, so I remember on some occasions, going to dinner with his seminary friends. Everyone at the table either had a master's degree or was working on one. I was the only one who didn't. As a result, I felt like the dumb one in the room. Whenever I would speak, I was also the controversial one so I would ask questions that nobody would ask, or I would say things that were just too provocative to say. Dharius would nudge me under the table as a sign that I shouldn't speak. But when he nudged me, I thought he was calling me dumb. I thought he was trying to silence me because I wasn't smart enough. The truth is, he was trying to protect me. He didn't want people to see me as the controversial wife. He was right to signal to me, "babe, rethink how you say that because your words can be taken out of context," but in my mind, I felt like the uneducated woman. Even when he began working at his first ministry assignment, Dharius started as a youth pastor and quickly became the interim pastor of a church. When he was promoted to interim pastor, I started teaching the youth and young adults in his place. Immediately, I felt like people were comparing my style to his style. Members would express, time and time again, that I wasn't doing it the way they thought it should be done. When he became the pastor of that church, it got even worse!

> In comparison to Dharius, I didn't feel smart enough. I didn't feel like anyone paid me any attention.

He was the pastor and by default, I was the First Lady. I didn't go to school for this! We were 22 years old and there were so many expectations of a first lady that I just didn't understand. Remember, we were young, and we were newly married. I wore appropriate clothes to church considering my age. But the older women at the church told me I wasn't dressed like a first lady. In fact, one of the members (we'll call her Ms. C.), God bless her soul, pulled me to the side one Sunday after church and told me, "That attire is not first lady attire." Ms. C. even took me to New York to buy me hats and suits that were more "first lady appropriate." The only problem was, these hats and suits were made for women in their fifties and sixties. I didn't know how to tell her "thank you, but no thank you." My insecurities taught me that if they said I needed to wear it, then I needed to wear it…so that's what I did.

When it came time for me to step into leadership roles at the church, I got criticized for every little thing. I inherited a women's ministry, for example, that voted on everything. They voted on flowers. They voted on who would give the theme for women's day. They voted on the color that everyone would wear. To me, that wasn't the purpose of women's ministry. So when I began to lead, we stopped the voting and I invited a powerhouse speaker to a one night women's gathering. I wanted our women to have a breakthrough experience and to learn how to love the Lord and develop a more consistent devotional life. I started a women's bible study and a praise dance ministry. Well, that didn't fly too well with one of the sisters who called me at work one day to let me have it. When I answered the phone, I was open to receiving her feedback. When I hung up the phone, I was in tears. She tore me to pieces telling me what I should and shouldn't do. She told me that I was wrong to come in and take over the ministry the way I did, and if I had any esteem left, trust me, it was completely erased by the time I hung up that phone. Overwhelmed by all of this, I called my husband to tell him what happened. And I'll never forget what he said because that was the first time I heard the acronym O.H.I.O—a phrase we currently use at our church to train leaders. O.H.I.O. means "only handle it once." That's what my husband told me to do. He told me that I had lost my center. I had thrown away the aggressive parts of me because I thought being saved meant to be passive. But he assured me that being saved did not mean that I was passive, and he encouraged me to handle it once, have a courageous conversation with those women, and lead to the best of my ability. He said exactly what I needed to hear, and I did exactly what he told me to do. That day, I decided not to wear another big hat or big suit. I kindly told the women "thank you for your recommendations, but this is how we will proceed." I picked myself up off of the floor, and I began to rise into the woman that I am today.

## RISE UP!

*Your hands have made and fashioned me; give me understanding that I may learn your commandments.*

–Psalms 119:73 -(ESV)

I don't know when that breaking point will happen for you, but in order to rise from insecurity, you've got to decide that enough is enough. Enough crying over spilled milk. Enough apologizing for who you are. Enough walking on egg shells. Enough lowering your standards for acceptance. Enough asking people for permission to be you! Enough! One day, I had had enough. It felt like I was always trying to fit into shoes that were too small for me. I can't tell you how many times insecurity caused full-out arguments in my home because whenever my husband tried to give me constructive criticism, I interpreted his help as hurt. I interpreted his recommendations as disapproval. The enemy wants you to believe that people sent to your life to help you are there to hurt you. But you've got to decide that enough is enough. The day insecurity will lose its hold from your life is when you ACKNOWLEDGE where you are. I had to take off the blinders and admit that I didn't feel as if I was enough. I had to acknowledge that I looked for positions, people, and platforms to **validate** me because I felt like the problem in every situation. As you acknowledge your insecurities, I also want to recommend an activity I learned from a mentor. Find yourself in Scripture. Find a biblical character that matches where you are, or how you feel. That Biblical character may not be a female if you're a

> *Every woman has a breaking point where they decide, "enough is enough."*

female, or a male if you're a male, but when you look at their life, find something that is similar to yours. Reading the book of Esther helped me to acknowledge what I was truly feeling. Esther was given another name when she was born, Hadassah, but for most of her life, she is responding to a name that others have given her. Eventually, she became a Jewish queen so there is value in Esther, but the road she had to take in order to understand her value came with a lot of twists and turns. Esther was an orphan who felt misplaced all of her life. She lived with her cousin Mordecai, and she was instrumental in delivering people by going to the king on their behalf. She was giving. She was loving. But the "TV family connection" was not there. Mordecai cared for her, but I believe she was longing for something Mordecai couldn't give her. She was also beautiful to look upon, and instead of praising her beauty, she became an inmate of the palace. When Vashti wasn't "picked at the social event," Esther became the second-runner up. Her place in the palace reversed everything for the Jews, but it came at a high cost. When I thought about Esther, it helped me to identify with some of the parallels of my life. Acknowledging where you are is important because it points you to where you're going.

After I acknowledged where I was, I then began to UNCOVER the truth by identifying the root. The root of my issue was that I had a false sense of reality. I assumed that the images I saw on TV were true, and the life I lived in reality was a lie. The root issue was that I needed someone to tell me I was enough before I believed it myself. I needed someone to tell me I was smart before I believed it myself. The root issue was that I didn't know to ask for help because I didn't know I needed it. The lies I told myself were that I would never be the girl someone would pick at the social event. I would never match up to my husband's brilliance. I would never be "first lady" material. I would never be considered smart to the world unless I earned a master's degree. These were all lies. The truth was—with a degree or without a degree—I was valuable. With a man or without a man, I was enough. With children or without them, I was chosen. I was fashioned by God's hands. He made me intentionally. He made me uniquely. He took his time when He designed me. His love for me was proven in the people he sent to me. He sent people to next-level me. He sent challenges to sharpen me. He sent experiences to strengthen my faith in him. Every time I thought I would fall, He showed me by his grace that I was His child.

Jesus specializes in uncovering our truth. In John 4, the Samaritan woman approached Jesus at the well. He asks her for a drink of water, and they begin to talk. As they talk, Jesus uncovers the truth of her insecurity. This woman had been searching for living water in human relationships. She was looking for men to fill her up, and Jesus kindly put an end to her longing by exposing the root of her issue. Maybe she was lonely. Maybe she was damaged. Maybe she had a "TV version of marriage" that didn't work out, so she kept trying until she gave up. Five husbands later, she's still searching for living water. Maybe her insecurity was due to hidden abandonment issues. We don't know for sure, but what we do know is that one encounter with Jesus changes her life forever. When we allow Jesus to uncover our truth, the truth sets us free. We can then go into the town and tell the world, "Come see a man who told me everything I ever did." This process is not easy, but it is certainly worth it. The truth was, I felt very similar to that woman in John 4. But when I allowed Jesus to fill me with his living water, with the Word, and with purpose, I was able to take baby steps out of insecurity and into security in Him.

After I uncovered my truths, I then had to EXAMINE the side-effects of insecurity. If I allowed insecurity to stay, my children would be born with the same issues. If I allowed insecurity to stay, I would never be able to trust that people would keep their word. If I allowed insecurity to stay, I would never have been able to lead the way God called me to lead. The primary side-effect of insecurity is comparison. When you are truly insecure, you will compare your life to someone else and aim to become someone that you are not. You also tend to micromanage, control, and resign easily. Micromanagement stems from the fact that you can't control what you can't control, so you must control what you can control. Resignation happens when you give up the moment you experience a little opposition. The moment it sounds like they aren't interested in you. The moment they expose the parts of you that you've been trying to hide, you run in the opposite direction. How long will you let insecurity rule your life? How long will you allow the side-effects to grow weeds in your garden? It's easy to give up when you don't feel worthy enough to apply for the job. It's easy to give up when you see yourself as the last resort, and not God's perfect choice. When I realized that the side-effects of insecurity were too heavy for me to carry on my own, I then gained the power to ARISE and make the change.

The Bible says I am fearfully and wonderfully made. I had always heard that Scripture, but one day I brought that Scripture into my prayer room. As a person who loves to journal, I began to write my prayer to God. Here is a little excerpt of what I discovered that day in His presence:

> During my healing process, I learned that I was not perfect but I was perfected for who God created me to be.

*God, as I sit here and look at how beautiful you've made everything around me I think about how you were so detailed in all that you created. If you did this for the ocean, the sand, the, sky, and the sea animals, then I know you did the same in making me.*

*You took your time and made me so detailed: my mind, my heart, my body, my personality. It's all fearfully and wonderfully made by you. I'm grateful, thankful and appreciative. There are times that I am insecure and I don't always understand why I am the way I am, but in situations like these—you show me who I am and why I'm so unique.*

*I cannot hide who I am. I need to step out like a Lioness and roar. For me, roaring means to take the world, to stand up and pursue what you have called me to do, to walk it now and not just talk it. It's time to hear me roar.*

Maybe you should try praying from your heart and writing it down. Maybe you need to find a verse that helps you to make the change, and stand on that verse all year. Many women battle with insecurity but the key to your freedom is when you realize how strategic God is. God does everything well. As a part of his creation, you are not just good…you are very good! Every day you get up, I want you to remind yourself that God's grace is sufficient. He will work strength out of your weakness. I did that and I started to see real change in my life. Slowly but surely, I was able to reclaim my power. I took off other people's expectations of me, and started to accept the person God made me to be. David would've never defeated Goliath with Saul's armor. I had to remove the armor that other people said was "the way" and I had to ask God to fashion me the way he needed me to be fashioned. *Teach me how to speak. Teach me how to love. Teach me how to accept compliments. Teach me how to receive criticism. Bring people into my life that will help me to improve. Please don't let me push people away those who are meant to stay; and please don't let me keep people in my life who are supposed to leave.* I made the change when I started to really believe that I was enough. Flaws and all, God made me who I am for a reason, and I am enough. You, too, are enough. You are fearfully and wonderfully made. You are special in God's eyes, and the world is a better place because you're here.

# RISE UP!

1. Acknowledge: take off the blinders

2. Uncover: identify the root – replace the lie.

3. Examine: evaluate the side-effects of insecurity

4. Arise: Make the Change

*I will not let my past keep me stuck. I will not focus on my weaknesses. Instead, I will remember that God's grace is sufficient. I will remind myself that even though I am not perfect, I have been perfected in Christ for everything he has called me to do.*

2 Corinthians 12:9 ESV – But he said to me, "My grace is sufficient for you, for my power is made perfect in weakness." Therefore I will boast all the more gladly of my weaknesses, so that the power of Christ may rest upon me.

*Whenever I need to be built up in life, I will lean on God. For he is my confidence and strength. In Him I receive encouragement and hope. He gives me the power to face whatever has been presented to me.*

Hebrews 4:16 ESV – Let us then walk with confidence. Draw near to the throne of grace, that we may receive mercy and find grace to help in the time of need.

## PRAYER

God, I am so grateful that you have created me uniquely. Help me to embrace and love the person you have created me to be. Whenever I get discouraged and whenever I started to question myself, Lord help me to accept who you've made me to be. Help me to see myself the way that you see me. From this day forward, I will trust you. I know that you created me for a reason and I won't allow the enemy to make me think otherwise. You are my strength. You are my encouragement. I am fearfully and wonderfully made. Amen.

# CHAPTER 3

# ARISE FROM FEAR

*For God gave us a spirit not of fear but of power and love and self-control.*

—2 Timothy 1:7 (ESV)

Every morning, on my way to school, my mother made me recite two scriptures from memory. One of those scriptures was 2 Timothy 1:7- *God has not given us the spirit of fear. But of power, love, and self-control.* Those words were ingrained in my psyche as a child. Those words were so familiar to me, it was like saying my first and last name. My mother was adamant about teaching me the Word of God, so I knew the language of faith. I knew the verse by heart. I was clear about what God had given me, but I was not experiencing power, love, or self-control in my life. Fear told me what to do. All throughout my childhood, the fingerprints of fear showed up in just about every scene of my life. The first thing I feared was failure. I was afraid of not doing well. So, I woke up early, I stayed up late. I read books over

*Instead, I was gripped by fear. Fear was my employer. Fear was my principal.*

and over again not because I enjoyed them, but because I was afraid to fail. If I got a 95% on a test, I immediately looked for what I did wrong so that I wouldn't do it again. It got so bad that as an adult, I added a wake-up chime to my alarm clock that said, "failure is not an option." Those were the words I woke up to every morning because I wanted to succeed at everything. But, the truth is, those words weren't helping me…they were hurting me.

Sometimes, we say things like "failure is not an option," or "I'll sleep when I die," as motivational tools to inspire us, but they actually become stumbling blocks that can hinder us. Sometimes, we read quotes on social media that sound inspirational in the moment, but when we try to apply that recommendation into our lives, it isn't realistic. It doesn't help us. The truth is, failure happens to us all. Mistakes will happen. Sleep is necessary. Anyone who lives without sleep is not making healthy choices. They are trying to be something that God didn't create them to be. If God didn't want us to rest, He would've made us robots. But he didn't. And for a long time, I set the bar so high in my life that I made it impossible for me to succeed. I was more than overachiever. I determined my value by how well I did in school, at work, or in my life. Eventually, this unrealistic expectation caused me to crash. I was hard to live with because I was projecting my expectations of success onto everyone I loved. The root of all of this was fear. What if I don't pass? What if no one loves me? What if I don't get the job? As long as fear reigned and ruled my life, I would never be who God called me to be. Why?

I know this is true because I always wanted to be a doctor growing up. It was my lifelong dream to be a nurse or a physician. Everyone who asked me about my career choices in high school knew that. My plan was to major in biology in college, study as a pre-med student, and apply for med school in the end. But fear froze my dreams after my first semester. Beyond the fear of failure, I also had a fear of death and dying. I was OK with treating patients who were sick, but I felt uncomfortable about treating patients who were about to die. Of course, as a doctor, I would have to encounter death on a regular basis but I was fearful of death because of experiences that happened in my childhood. If you've ever been haunted by fear, gripped by fear, and controlled by fear, the first thing I need you to do is go back to the root. Where did this fear come from? When did it start impacting your decisions? Why has it become a hindrance to you?

I've learned not to judge what I don't understand, and I've met many people who are afraid of many things—some people are afraid of dogs and others are afraid of the dark. But when they go back to the root, they realize where it all stems from. Maybe they were chased by a dog

> Because fear has the power to keep you from certain opportunities, and fear loves to block you from going through certain doors.

as a child and the trauma of their past has imprisoned their future. So now, at the very mention or view of a dog, they tense up. They run in the opposite direction.

Others who are afraid of the dark may have experienced unwanted affection in the dark. The dark may represent a hidden secret in the family, or a robber breaking-in their home at night—so as adults, they've made a decision to sleep with the light on. For me, my fear of death began in the second grade. As a child, I connected with few people. But one student in my school, befriended me and very quickly, we became best friends. Our parents worked together. We had so much in common. We got along and I looked forward to hanging out with him in school every day. But one day, my buddy didn't come to school on time. I didn't think anything of it until the teacher walked in and announced that he had been in an accident. He was hit by a car and died on impact.

I was only 7 or 8 years old. I had no concept of death. I knew people died but no one close to me had passed away. When my friend died suddenly, I didn't know how to reconcile his death, deal with loss, and process my grief. So, fear became the counterfeit comforter. It became something that hovered over me like a cloud. I knew I was sad, but I swept my pain under the rug and I cried about it behind closed doors. I immediately ran to fear instead of turning to God. From that moment on, I became very afraid of losing people I loved. But what I have learned about life is that unaddressed issues always show up again as cycles.

Five years later, I was now in the seventh grade, and the same thing happened. I became close with another friend. He and I talked on the phone every day. We were really tight and we laughed about everything. The last we spoke, he told me he was going swimming and I expected a call from him that night when he got home. But he never called. I didn't lose any sleep over it. I just thought it was out of the ordinary; until the next morning when I found out the truth. He drowned in the pool. Immediate death. Sudden loss. Again, I was confronted with death and I didn't know how to process it. So, I suppressed it. I became very clingy with some people (out of fear that I would lose them) or I became very transactional. I wouldn't allow myself to get too close because I didn't know if they would stay. Both options were problematic, but I decided to live under the false reality of pretense. I never confronted my pain. I just acted like I was fine. Then, like clockwork, it happened again.

Before I turned 18, I had lost three close friends, and over time, these losses turned into a deep-seeded fear. I did not go to funerals. I avoided talking about death. I wouldn't watch

*Now three years later, during high school, my God-sister was killed by a drunk driver.*

television shows with dead people or dying patients. Out of sight, out of mind was my coping mechanism. And ultimately, I changed my major in college because I just couldn't risk someone dying in front of me, on the operating table. Do you see how my entire life was reshaped by fear? I may have become the best doctor in town, but my private phobia had public repercussions. It almost controlled my entire life, but one day, God forced me to rise from fear and face my issues. The beginning of my turnaround happened when I married a man who became a pastor.

As a pastor, my husband had to deal with loss all of the time. We had to visit the sick, pray for their families, counsel grieving families through loss, and eulogize our members who passed away. As the first lady, I had no choice but to face my fear head-on. *God had not given me the spirit of fear, but of power, love, and self-control.* Those words started to take root in my life, and I would speak that scripture before every conversation I had with a grieving member. Over time, I learned how to process my fear in a healthy manner, and eventually, I decided to address it as soon as I felt it creeping up on me.

If your issues are not addressed, the cycle will continue. Don't let anyone tell you that it would be better to say nothing at all than to tell the truth about how you feel. That is false. The truth will set you free. Even if the truth is hard to admit, freedom is on the other side of truth. But silence will only breed secrecy. Secrecy will only breed deception, and deception will eventually bring death (spiritual death and emptiness). Not only will you deceive others, but you will start to deceive yourself. When I truly began to admit my fears, and identify the root of my fears, I felt a weight lift off of me. I literally felt like fear had me under a bench press, and the more I ignored it, the heavier the weight became. But I learned to get control over my thoughts by talking to God about everything (and I do mean everything). The moment a contrary thought would come to mind, I would cancel that fear, and focus on the truth of God's word.

Your fear may not be death. Your fear may be something else. Many people fear wasting time. Other people fear not being perfect. The top 10 fears that humans struggle with are as follows:

1. The fear of losing your freedom
2. The fear of the unknown
3. The fear of pain or experiencing pain
4. The fear of disappointment
5. The fear of misery
6. The fear of loneliness
7. The fear of ridicule
8. The fear of rejection
9. The fear of death
10. The fear of failure

What I've learned is that everyone fears something— so the question is not, do you fear anything; the question is what do you fear? The hardest part is to acknowledge what you're fearing. Don't act like it doesn't exist. Do you remember the man in the Bible who approached Jesus and said, "I believe but help my unbelief." All of us will have moments where we want to believe in something or someone, but we can't believe on our own. We are wrestling with fear. And sometimes, we can believe that God can do it for others, but we don't believe that God can do it for us.

When you are ready to rise from fear, you must first ACKNOWLEDGE. I had to acknowledge everything that held me back from being the woman God made me. I remember applying to graduate school, after taking a long hiatus, and immediately, the fear of failure popped up again. This time, fear was saying I wasn't smart enough to ace these classes. I had taken too much time off. I wouldn't be able to finish school, and if I did, I would need someone else to write my papers for me. For a quick second, I allowed my mind to believe the lies, and I started to reach out to friends for help.

Asking for help was fine, but underneath my request for help was the fear that I couldn't do it on my own. I didn't know if I could do the work, manage my life, and succeed without someone else. Eventually, I stopped spiraling into negative thoughts. I stopped doubting my own abilities, and I decided that if God called me to it, He would help me through it. The first paper I turned in without anyone else's help, I aced the paper! I can't tell you how accomplished I felt in that moment. God used that semester to show me that I was capable. I was qualified. I was called to do this. I didn't have to depend on people to get the work done with me. I needed to trust that I was enough, and if I needed to ask for help, I would do so knowing it wasn't because of something that was innately wrong with me.

In the same way, I want you to acknowledge what you are afraid of. I want you to tell the truth to yourself, about yourself. What do you fear and why do you fear it? Then, I want you to UNCOVER the reality by identifying the root. The root, for me, happened when I was in the second grade. When did fear introduce itself to you? Did fear walk in when someone else walked out? What is the root cause of your fears? Has it kept you from succeeding? Has it hindered your growth?

When I looked up the definition of fear, I learned that fear is a feeling induced by a perceived danger or threat. What feelings have supported your fear? What signs or memories make you feel like you are in danger? You are smart enough. You don't need someone else to do your work. You are going to become a doctor. You are going to be a great mother. You don't have to change your major just because you are afraid of death. You are sound. You are strong. You are capable. You are enough. The lie I consistently told myself was that people I loved would

> As you begin to identify the root, you must also replace the lie.

die unexpectedly. But the truth is, God is not surprised by loss. God knows who will transition and when they will transition, and when they go, he has promised never to leave me or forsake me. The truth is, my definition comes from Him. My purpose comes from Him. God is the author and finisher of my faith, and anything He has called me to, he will help me to accomplish.

After I replaced the lies, then I had to EXAMINE the side-effects of fear. When fear controls your life, purpose becomes dormant. Fear freezes productivity. Fear compromises your destiny. The side-effects of fear include procrastination, excuses, regret, unfinished tasks, and paranoia. People who allow fear to control their decisions are always over-thinking and under-producing. But when you RISE from the grip of fear, you can stabilize your emotions by taking authority over your mind. You can turn fear upside down and use it as a motivator instead of as a hindrance. One writer said it this way, "Fear is that little dark room where negatives are developed." This quote has helped me to see fear for what it can produce in my life. When I bring my fears to God, he can recycle my negatives and turn them into positives. When I bring my nervousness to God, he can take my discomfort and turn it into courage. When I cast my cares on him, He can relieve me in His presence and assure me that everything is going to be alright. But God can't transform what we refuse to surrender. The only way to fight fear is to admit what you're afraid of. One day, you're going to have to surrender your fears to the only one who can help you overcome. When you arise from fear and make the change, you will surrender control of those things you can't control. You will let go of the past, and focus on the future. When we give our fears to God, God can turn those fears into faith. Today, admit your fears to the Lord. He already knows what you need. But He wants you to let it go so he can take control.

## RISE UP!

1. Acknowledge: take off the blinders

2. Uncover: identify the root – replace the lie.

3. Examine: evaluate the side-effects of fear

4. Arise: Make the Change

*Psalm 23:4 ESV*

*Even though I walk through the valley of the shadow of death, I will fear no evil, for you are with me; your rod and your staff, they comfort me.*

When feelings of fear try to overwhelm me, I will remind myself that it doesn't matter what is going on or where I am-- God is with me. Many of us fear being alone but God has a way of teaching us to find our trust in him. When we find our trust in Him, it will comfort us and give us the courage to overcome. You can overcome fear. You don't have to live captive to its stronghold. But trusting God is the prerequisite.

*Joshua 1:9 ESV*

*Have I not commanded you? Be strong and courageous. Do not be frightened, and do not be dismayed, for the LORD your God is with you wherever you go."*

When fear creeps in, stand on God's word. Be obedient to what He has commanded. Be strong and courageous.

## PRAYER

God, I thank you for your word and your promise. Thank you for always being with me. There are times when my faith is weak and I allow fear to flare up. Help me to get to the root of my fear so that I can be strong and courageous. I know I am not the only one that can access the self control that I need to overcome. I love you and I trust you. Amen.

# CHAPTER 4

# ARISE FROM CONDITIONAL LOVE

*Love is patient and kind; love does not envy or boast; it is not arrogant or rude. It does not insist on its own way; it is not irritable or resentful; it does not rejoice at wrongdoing, but rejoices with the truth. Love bears all things, believes all things, hopes all things, endures all things. Love never ends. As for prophecies, they will pass away; as for tongues, they will cease; as for knowledge, it will pass away.*

—1 Corinthians 13:4-8

LOVE. It's one of the most popular words used in our society today. We tell our children "I love you" as they leave the house before school. We sign the words "I love you" on anniversary cards and handwritten letters. We hang up the phone with close friends, and before we say goodbye, you'll often hear "I love you." Love is a word that everyone has used, but most people mean something entirely different when they say it. I know for me, as a child, I saw love as protection, affection, and provision. I didn't have a scriptural understanding of love when I was a child. I had an image in my head that I wanted to see in my life. If someone loved me, they wouldn't harm me. If someone loved me, they would show affection toward me. They would hold my hand. They would open the door for me. They would hug me. They would take care of me. That was my definition of love, so that was what I desired. I didn't just desire this kind of love from my parents, I also desired this kind of love from other people. So, I searched for love like a Where's Waldo picture book. Everywhere I went, I needed to experience love. I needed to find love. I'm sure my issues of rejection and insecurity played into my never-ending search for love, but I didn't know then what I know now.

I remember dating someone that I thought really loved me. But when I evaluated the relationship after it ended, I realized that his love toward me was based on conditions. *I'll do this for you if you do that for me. I'll go here with you if you go there with me.* Have you ever found yourself in a conditional relationship? Even if it was a friendship, have you ever been in relationship with someone who was a tit-for-tat kind of friend? Maybe they enjoyed your company, and maybe they appreciated your time, but in the end, they always had a motive attached to their expectation of you? That is conditional love. This kind of love isn't bad necessarily, but it wasn't the love I was looking for. I

Conditional love is when someone gives you love based on what you do.

didn't want to audition for love. I didn't want to feel like someone would leave me if they saw my scars. I wanted to be loved, flaws and all. I now have language for it. What I was looking for was unconditional love.

Much different than conditional love, unconditional love is a kind of love given to you, no matter what you do. That means, despite your behavior, your hang-ups or your mistakes, unconditional love is here to stay. Unconditional love will travel the distance with you. When someone loves you unconditionally, they love you "to infinity and beyond."

Life quickly taught me that most people love you conditionally, and only a few will love you unconditionally. My conditional friends were nice people. They enjoyed being around me. I enjoyed being around them. But if I didn't meet their spoken or unspoken expectations of me, I'd notice a shift in our bond. The same was true with my romantic relationships. Most people are always on their best behavior in the beginning. In college, I dated this one guy who met my criteria of love (or so I thought). He was protective, he was affectionate, and he spent time with me. I received everything I needed in the beginning, but as the relationship continued, the love changed. He became short with me and impatient with me. I felt like I was being tolerated and not celebrated. He didn't care a lot about things that happened in my life but he wanted me to care deeply about things happening in his. Slowly but surely, he became abusive. He became abusive with my time, my space, and my freedom. I told myself that love sticks it out until the end, so I put myself in compromising situations that triggered my rejection and insecurity issues. I didn't realize it at the time, but I was allowing him to be emotionally abusive and verbally abusive, and instead of confronting him, I just made up excuses for his behavior. *He had a rough day. He will be alright by tomorrow.* I began to settle. I began to ignore the red flags.

> Whenever you are unaware of God's best for you, you will accept the worst and settle for less.

One day, I saw that his emotional abuse and verbal abuse was on the brink of becoming physical abuse, so I ended the relationship. I didn't know the difference between conditional love and unconditional love at the time, so I settled.

When I met Dharius, I experienced something different. I didn't call it unconditional love at the time, but I quickly noticed that he wasn't like other guys. He didn't walk away when I did something he didn't like. Instead, he loved me through my issues. He didn't make me audition for his affection. Instead, he unlocked parts of my heart that I didn't even know were closed off. At some point during our dating chapter, I remember asking Dharius to show me love. I couldn't even define what I wanted but I continued to ask for it. At first I thought I needed him to become more affectionate. Then I thought I needed him to be more affirming. Later, I felt like I needed him to spend quality time with me. None of those things filled me up, so I started to ask him to take me on more dates. He did everything I asked him to do, but I didn't feel fulfilled. Something was missing. Something was wrong. He was giving me everything I thought I wanted, and it still wasn't enough.

Then, like a light switch being turned on, I realized the problem. I was a broken glass asking someone to pour into me. If you've ever tried to fill a cracked glass, you understand what I mean. When I thought about my life as an insecure child, as a rejected child, and as a hurt child, I realized

> Cracked glasses can be poured into, but they can't be filled. They can receive fluid, but they can't contain it.

that it was impossible for one man to do what only God could do. Dharius could love me, but only God could heal me. I needed God to patch up the holes of my heart and to fix the cracked places of my life in order for me to be filled to capacity.

If you're like me and you've had a difficult past, let me encourage you. You may have been damaged but you are not destroyed. You may have been broken but you are not beyond repair. God can patch up your holes. God can repair your broken places. God can fill the void, and if you open yourself to his unconditional love, He will heal parts of you that you didn't even know were broken. You can try to find fulfillment in a friendship or in a relationship, but only God can fix this. There is not enough money, pleasure, attention, promotion, or power that can satisfy the longing in your soul. I needed unconditional love. I needed God. I needed to stop searching for man to do what only God could do. I needed to turn the page and accept that if God never sent me a husband, I could still be filled by Him. And if God never blessed me with children, I could still be filled by Him.

I was a broken glass looking for others to fill me; and the thing about broken glasses is this—we know how to give love but we don't know how to receive it. The broken areas of my past made it hard for me to receive. Nevertheless, I decided to RISE.

## RISE UP!

Rising in this area required a change in my definition of love. Love was *not* the image I grew up longing for as a child. Love was exactly what the Bible says it is in 1 Corinthians 13:

> *Love is patient and kind; love does not envy or boast; it is not arrogant or rude. It does not insist on its own way; it is not irritable or resentful; it does not rejoice at wrongdoing, but rejoices with the truth. Love bears all things, believes all things, hopes all things, endures all things. Love never ends. As for prophecies, they will pass away; as for tongues, they will cease; as for knowledge, it will pass away.*

God began to teach me what love *was*, by showing me what love *was not*. The first word used to define love in 1 Corinthians 13 is patience. Love doesn't rush you. Instead, love will wait for you to grow into who God has called you to be. Love is also kind. That means, love doesn't hurt. Love doesn't manipulate. Love is caring and love is thoughtful. As well, love does not envy or boast. When I read this, I realized that conditional lovers will tell everyone what they did for you so they can get public affirmation. But unconditional love doesn't brag about the sacrifices it makes for you. It doesn't "throw shade" at you in private, and then blow kisses to you in public. Unconditional love is not jealous of you. In fact, it is impossible for someone to love you if they are jealous of you. They may like you, but they cannot love you. *Love is not arrogant or rude.* When unconditional love speaks to you, it doesn't puff itself up. It does not verbally use you. It always thinks about how to say difficult things in the most thoughtful manner. Love seasons all conversations with grace. *Love does not insist on its own way.* Have you ever been in a relationship with someone who insists on driving to the store the way they want to go, eating at this restaurant, paying the bills the way they want to do it? Love doesn't insist on its own way. Instead, unconditional love is a compromise. Sometimes, we will do it my way and sometimes we will do it your way. *Love is not irritable or resentful.* This means that love doesn't make you feel like

> If there are people in your life who will rejoice when you fall but keep silent when you succeed, here's a hard truth: they don't love you.

you have to walk on eggshells. Love doesn't get easily offended. Offense may come, but unconditional love will listen quickly and speak slowly. *Love does not rejoice at wrongdoing but rejoices in the truth.* In other words, real love is not rejoicing when you fall. Real love isn't silently smirking when you fail. Unconditional love *bears all things, hopes all things, endures all things. Unconditional love never ends.* Whenever I read those words, I can't help but to think about my husband. He constantly pushed me toward hope even when I wanted to focus on the hurt. He has endured seasons when I would constantly ask him for love—even when I didn't know what I was asking for. His love for me does not come with stipulations. As an imperfect woman, I mess up. I make mistakes. I don't know what I would do if my husband walked away every time I made a mistake. In the same way, God didn't just reveal his unconditional love for me through prayer. He also revealed his love for me through people.

When you begin to rise from conditional love, God will bring people into your life who will show you God's love in human form. They are living, breathing demonstrations of God's unconditional love. Thank God for friends who love me through it all. Thank God for ride-or-die family members who don't judge me when I fall. Thank God for a husband who didn't see the cracks in my glass and stop pouring. Instead, he continued to give his all even when I could only receive some.

My encouragement to you is to build your foundation with a revelation of God's never-ending love. God's love does not come with conditions. He doesn't stop loving you because you messed up. He doesn't love you any less when you do something you shouldn't have done. God won't abuse you. He won't take your heart and misuse you. Instead, God's mercy and grace endures. God gives us what we don't deserve and he withholds from us what we do deserve. The love of God is an endless river of peace and joy. God's love will secure you. God's love will heal you from the inside out. When I truly began to embrace the love of God, I stopped looking for people to do what only God can do. I began to accept the gift of love that others were trying to give me. Most importantly, I was able to give that same unconditional love to others.

I see it so clearly now that I have children. I love my children unconditionally. In my mind, they can do no wrong, but all parents know, our children make mistakes, too. Dharius and I have two sons—Seth and Gabe. Our oldest son, Seth, is a spitting image of me but he acts like his father. Our youngest son, Gabe, is a spitting image of his father but he acts like me. One day, Seth was coming home from basketball practice. He wanted to have company over, but he knew the rules: don't ask if people can come over while they are in the car with you on the way to our home. Before you get in the car, call us, have a conversation, and then, after we make a decision, communicate our decision to your friends. Of course, Seth didn't do that. While the kids were listening to Seth, he called me. As his mom, I had two choices. Do I revert to the "old Shameka" and reprimand him loudly over the phone? Or do I handle this situation differently? I'm now very aware of the fact that Seth's friends look up to him and they look up to his parents. They know who we are and what we do, so anything I say can be used against me! I politely and calmly told Seth we would talk about it when he got home.

Once he arrived, I pulled him to the side and I asked him to reiterate the rules. At this point, his friends were in our home but I wanted to make sure we talked so that we could avoid a future pattern. Seth told me the rules and he was clear that he broke them. I asked him why. He told me that one child didn't get picked up from practice and he didn't want to leave him there alone. Seth was actually being thoughtful of the child who didn't have a ride, and he didn't want that child to feel excluded so he invited all of his friends over to our home. I didn't know this when he called. And I would've probably done the same thing Seth did.

Now imagine if I had scolded him without getting all of the information? He was doing what we taught him to do—to care for those who can't care for themselves and to extend kindness when you see that someone is in need.

Sure, his actions didn't fall within the guidelines that we set as his parents, but when he explained what happened, I understood why he did what he did. In that moment, I was able to extend love to him the way others had extended love to me.

Don't you see how your freedom from conditional love can impact everyone around you? In order to experience God's best in the love area, first we have to ACKNOWLEDGE what is going on around us. I was so blinded by the image of love that I created in my mind, that I was not aware of the love God was trying to show me. I had to take off the blinders and ask God to reveal love to me from His word, not from my head. Then, I had to UNCOVER the patterns that kept me from receiving love. I did that by identifying the root of my problem. The root was that I didn't love myself. And when you don't love yourself, you will always discount your worth. I didn't see myself as the Scriptures saw me. I didn't see myself as a priceless treasure. The lies I told myself were: *accept what you've been given. You probably won't get anything better than this.* Or, I told myself, *you don't deserve unconditional love because you've made too many mistakes in your past.* Whatever lie you've told yourself, decide today that you will replace the lie with the truth. God loves you so much that he gave his only son for you. He literally sent Jesus into this world, to take your place on the cross. Jesus laid down his life so you wouldn't have to. There is no greater love than

*God loves you unconditionally. He loves you without pre-existing conditions.*

this. He loves you without fine print disclaimers. There is nothing you can do to earn more of God's love, and there is nothing you can do to lose it. If you went to church every day, He'd love you just the same. If you stopped reading your Bible and if you made some bad decisions, He'd love you just the same. His love is not based on human effort. His love is based on grace. He loves you fully, abundantly, and overwhelmingly. This is the truth of God's love.

After you accept the truth, then you must EXAMINE the side-effects of conditional love. These side-effects include never being satisfied with who you are, never feeling as if you are enough, always living as if you are auditioning for acceptance, always giving so that others can return the favor. Conditional love only works for perfect people. But when you are imperfect, you feel as if you can't give or receive what you don't deserve. Listen: that's not your responsibility. You can ARISE today and make the change. I made the change when I allowed God to fill my broken places. I made the change when I learned to not just give love but to receive it. I made the change when I decided not to let temporary emotions cloud my judgment. I, Shameka Daniels, am loved by God. And you (INSERT YOUR NAME) are loved by God. He is madly in love with you and He will continue to love you in every season of your life.

# RISE UP!

1. Acknowledge: take off the blinders

2. Uncover: identify the root – replace the lie.

3. Examine: evaluate the side-effects of conditional love.

4. Arise: Make the Change

## SCRIPTURES

*I John 11-4:7 ESV, Beloved, let us love one another, for love is from God, and whoever loves has been born of God and knows God. Anyone who does not love does not know God, because God is love. In this the love of God was made manifest among us, that God sent his only Son into the world, so that we might live through him. In this is love, not that we have loved God but that he loved us and sent his Son to be the propitiation for our sins. Beloved, if God so loved us, we also ought to love one another.*

God's love has taught me how to give and receive love. God loves us regardless of who we are, regardless of what we do, regardless of where we've been, and regardless of what we say. That is unconditional love. My relationship with God has opened my heart to love others unconditionally. As you read the scripture above, ask yourself, "What type of love have I given to those whom I have confessed to love? Conditional or unconditional?"

*Psalm 4-63:3 ESV*

*Because your steadfast love is better than life, my lips will praise you. So I will bless you as long as I live; in your name I will lift up my hands.*

Sometimes we get discouraged because we feel God's love but not the love of others around us. There are even times when we have to focus on God's love toward us and not the actions of others. In my prayer journal, I have learned to write all of God's promises to me and the reasons why he loves me. This helps me not to be distracted by others around me. When I pray and journal God's promises, it allows me to replace my thoughts with His truth. It also builds me up in his presence and I am able to sing praises to my God.

## PRAYER

God, your love is better than life and I will focus on your love toward me and not the actions of others. I will praise you and lift you up. God, I need your help every single day of my life. In the area of love, help me not to be distracted by those around me. Instead I want to focus on the good things that others do for me, and the path that you have directed me to focus on. I thank you for teaching me how to love and I thank you for loving me for me for who I am, as I am.

# CHAPTER 5

# ARISE FROM HURT

*Guard your heart with all vigilance, for from it flows the springs of life.*

—Proverbs 4:23 (ESV)

*He heals the brokenhearted and binds up their wounds*

—Psalms 147:3 (ESV)

*H*urt *people hurt people.* It's a fact. It's the truth. When someone is hurting, there is no language to describe the pain they feel. Certain levels of hurt are unexplainable. No matter how much backbone you have and no matter how resilient you are, hurt can break all of us. Hurt is something we wish we didn't have to experience. Whenever hurt comes knocking, we may look through the peephole to see who is on the other side, but once we see hurt for what it is, we will quickly turn around and act as if it came to the wrong home. *Hurt people hurt people.* The probability that hurting people will hurt someone else is high. When someone has been introduced to pain, mistreatment, neglect or abuse at a young age, they tend to project or inflict that pain onto others. Most times, it is unintentional. Other times it is intentional.

When I embraced my calling to help women find healing, I encountered countless women who told me they were still carrying hurt from their past. Some of these women were serving in the church. Some of these women were leading churches with their husbands, and some of these women were in their seventies and eighties.

*Meet Betty.* Betty was 13 years old when she first experienced intentional hurt. She was hanging out with her friend Sally after school. Like usual, they were planning to watch movies and chill until their parents came home from work. When the doorbell rang, Betty thought it was the pizza delivery guy. But Sally had invited two other guys over to the house. One was Sally's boyfriend, and the other was a friend of the boyfriend. Betty didn't like the idea of entertaining strangers but she went along with it to keep the peace. By the end of the night, Sally ended up in a private room with her boyfriend, and Betty ended up violated by a stranger. The stranger flirted throughout the evening and seemed to be a very understanding guy. But when Sally found herself alone with the stranger, he transformed into an aggressive maniac. Betty's been carrying this hurt for 50 years. She's never been intimate with a man since that time.

*Meet Abigail.* Abigail never met her father or her mother. While riding to a New Year's Eve service, her parents died in a car accident. She was the only survivor. Her aunts and uncles didn't want her. As a child, she was passed around from house to house like an unwanted piece of furniture. By the time she turned 21, she was a mother of five, by five different fathers. She thought she was in love with every boyfriend she had, but really, she was searching for her father in every man she met.

*Meet Violet.* Violet didn't find out she was adopted until she was finishing her PhD in Molecular Biology. Her advisor, Dr. Smith, recruited her to study at Penn State, and on the day she defended her dissertation, her advisor revealed that he was actually her brother. Violet was hurt for millions of reasons. First, she felt manipulated by her brother. Second, she didn't know that her parents weren't who they said they were. Third, she had more questions than answers, and no matter how smart she was, she'd always felt empty and disconnected from her family. Now she knew why. They didn't love her enough to tell the truth.

*Meet First Lady Malachi.* Every Sunday, she takes five more minutes to get out of bed. She hates church. She hates having to lie. She's been hurting for a long time, and this hurt is intentional. Her husband, Bishop Malachi, has been cheating on her for 15 years. In the beginning, it was painful. But now, she is numb. She's too deep in the marriage to leave. So she has decided to say nothing and do nothing. They have an agreement. Just don't come home with anything that will affect my physical wellbeing. Every

Sunday, she shows up right before the sermon. She nods. She smiles. She does her duties, and then she goes back home, and sleeps in the guest room.

*Feelings buried alive don't die.* Isn't it odd how we think we can cover up painful things like this? Isn't it interesting how trauma affects us all? I could go on and on about the shocking and difficult experiences I have heard over the last 12 years in ministry, but no matter the experience, the hurt leaves most people numb. Most people shut all the way down. They decide not to allow anything to affect them. They tell themselves that no one is worthy of trust, and they lose touch with feeling. They feel like a lifeless puppet. They either procrastinate to keep from living, or they overcompensate to expedite dying. The worst kind of pain is the one you can't tell because you're miserable but you're in ministry. Or, you're miserable but you're a mother. Or, you're miserable but you're a marketplace executive, and everyone expects you to fix their broken places.

All of these women have, at one point or another, sat down at a dinner table or in a healing workshop to talk through their pain. Most women will tell me they became guarded about everything. They were skeptical of everyone's motive. They were suspicious of their activity. They assumed the worst and never expected the best to happen. They were both paranoid and pessimistic. Others who didn't know the depth of their pain would call them rude, or conceited, but the truth is they were just hurting.

Can you relate to this? Maybe you haven't experienced the kind of pain listed above, but have you ever cut yourself off from yourself? Have you ever stood in a room and heard others talking to you? You nodded on the outside but you were lifeless on the inside. I know what that's like myself. I had experienced so much hurt before I turned 21, that at one point in my life, nothing affected me. If someone said they loved me, I didn't feel anything. I didn't feel butterflies of attraction, I didn't feel passion or pain—I felt nothing. I was burying my feelings in the grave of regret. I lost touch with who I was or what I was actually feeling. I felt trapped. I was trapped by what some people knew about me, and trapped by what others expected of me. I was trapped by the hurt I had to hide, and trapped by the hurt I had to protect. My unmet needs as a child caused me to reach out to others who did not have my best interest in mind. For a short season, I blamed everybody for the constant hurt I experienced. But the lesson I learned after processing my hurt, and after helping other women to process theirs is this: *what you sow in your past you may reap in your children.* Habits, patterns, and practices are all learned behaviors. My hurt, for example, became a magnet that attracted toxic people into my life. From guys who took my kindness for weakness, to the "sister-friend" I met in college. She and I were beyond close. If you know anything about me, you would know that I am a ride-or-die friend. When I get close to someone, I really get close. The same was true with this college friend. Her and I met when I was a sophomore and she was a freshman. We did everything together, and I affectionately called her my little sister. When she came into my life, I finally felt like I had the sister I never had. If she was in trouble, I bailed her out. If I did something crazy, she was right by my side.

But all of that changed when I shared a secret with her in confidence. I asked her to swear that she would keep this secret between us, and she told me she would. But before I got off the phone with her, it seemed as if my secret was told to half of the campus. Here I was again: hurt. I was hurt by the girl I called my sister. I was hurt by my "family member." That's what I told myself but that wasn't the truth. She wasn't my real sister. She wasn't my real family. But I told myself that because, when you are looking for others to fulfill an unmet need in you, you will give them roles in your life that aren't actually true. I trusted her as a sister so when she disappointed me, I didn't know how to shift my expectations. I applied familial expectations onto her that she couldn't keep—*don't hurt me if you love me*. She was wrong for what she did but I was wrong for expecting her to do more. Once again, trust was broken. My confidence in others was compromised, and I found myself suffering in silence.

If you're suffering in silence today, I want to encourage you with these words: what happened to you is not your fault. It took a long time for me to rise from self-blame and ridicule. I was inflicting more pain on my own soul every time I blamed myself for something I didn't deserve. I didn't ask for it. I didn't ask to be betrayed or to be taken advantage of. I didn't always know what to do, but the easiest thing was to blame myself.

Now that I've done the work to identify the root of my problem, I can say to you what I wish someone had said to me: it's not your fault. It's not your fault that you were not supported. It's not your fault that you experienced what you experienced. My husband always says, "God doesn't do everything but God will use everything." I never thought that I would one day have the courage to write a book about the hard truths of my life, but now I can see how God is using the misfortune of my past to reroute somebody else's future.

If you relate to Betty, Abigail, Violet, First Lady Malachi, or Shameka's story, hear me loud and hear me clear: this is not your fault, and you are not unfixable. You are not so broken that God cannot heal you. Sometimes, when we look at our experiences and we compare them to others, we don't always feel like God can do for us what he did for them. But God can do above what you ask or imagine. You will never be who God called you to be if you compare yourself to somebody else. Over time, God began to restore me. Over time, God brought people into my life so I could process the hidden stones in my heart. It didn't happen overnight, but it happened at the right time. What if today is your day...to rise?

## RISE UP!

*Guard your heart with all vigilance, for from it flows the springs of life.*

—Proverbs 4:23 (ESV)

*He heals the brokenhearted and binds up their wounds*

—Psalms 147:3 (ESV)

In the previous chapter, we spoke about God's unconditional love. Remember, God loves you unconditionally. His love is proven by what he does and by who he sends. Often, God will send people into your life who exemplify his love and care. A few years ago, God introduced me to a woman who became my mentor. When I first met her, I didn't realize what would happen over time. She helped me to uncover my wounds. She helped me to say what I couldn't say out loud. No one knew about the hurt I experienced, but at the right time, God sent me someone I could trust. This woman helped me to speak out. My silence was hurting me. But when I spoke out, I began to rise.

When I spoke out, I was able to ACKNOWLEDGE the reality. The reality was, I learned to put up walls to protect me from collateral damage. I put up a wall so I could stop myself from feeling. Have you ever put up walls in your heart? Maybe you weren't hurt like some of the ladies mentioned above were, but perhaps someone took advantage of you at work. So, you put up a wall and decided to never get close to another co-worker again. Many people are dating with walls, married with walls, having children with walls—and they believe that this is the best way to "guard their heart" from pain. But when the scripture says to "guard your heart" it is not saying to put up a wall. Instead, it is encouraging us to put up a gate instead of a wall. In other words, set up safe boundaries so that those who leave your life can't stay—and so that those who are called to stay in your life, can't leave. With gates, you can control who comes in and who goes out. With walls, everybody is out (even the people whom God sent to help you). The moment that clicked for me, I was able to rise from hurt. I was able to communicate better with my husband. I was able to extend grace to my children. I was able to trust again, and give people the same grace that God gave me. It took a lot of time, but with God all things are possible!

Today I have learned to protect my peace at all cost. I have also learned to use wisdom about those I bring close and those I keep a healthy distance from. Without question, I love everybody. But even Jesus had close friends, distant disciples, and colleagues in the crowd. Putting up a gate helped me to create clear boundaries for different people in my life. I teach at Change Church about knowing who is in your circle. When I began to put people where they belonged, I was able to protect myself from constant pain.

If you are tired of hurting, I want you to rise up and ACKNOWLEDGE where you are. Take off the blinders and confess some hard truths—I am hurt because_____. I put up a wall with _____. I lost trust in others when _____. The moment you take the blinders off, you'll be able to UNCOVER the truth by identifying the root. The root of my hurt was silence. I learned to be silent about my pain, and I assumed it would magically disappear. But it didn't. Sometimes, in order to break through you've got to speak up. What is the root cause of your hurt? What are the lies you've told yourself? Maybe you told yourself this was your fault. But the truth is, you didn't do anything wrong. You didn't cause this. Your parents didn't even cause this, or the person who hurt you—*this was the enemy.* He saw your future and wanted to destroy you early. He saw your destiny and wanted to ruin you forever. After you get clarity about that, then you can EXAMINE the side-effects of hurt, which include: fear, suppression, numbness, pretending, and codependency. If for no other reason, I want to encourage to ARISE for your children. ARISE for your parents. ARISE for your future. ARISE for the people God will send your way to encourage and counsel. ARISE today for what you can't see tomorrow. If hurt people hurt people, then whole people heal people.

# RISE UP!

1. Acknowledge: take off the blinders

2. Uncover: identify the root – replace the lie.

3. Examine: evaluate the side-effects of hurt.

4. Arise: Make the Change

   *Psalm 19-34:18 ESV*

   *The LORD is near to the brokenhearted and saves the crushed in spirit. Many are the afflictions of the righteous, but the LORD delivers him out of them all.*

   When we are hurting, the pain causes us to isolate, guard, and protect ourselves from never feeling that way again. But God's word tells us that He is near us even when we feel like He is not. This is the time we have to open up to God about how we feel and to allow him to heal our brokenness and deliver us out of it. The Bible does not suggest that this process will be easy. But it will be worth it: for there will be afflictions but God will deliver us out every time. Whenever you are in a season of pain, look to God and ask him what am I to learn out of this season? Have faith that he will heal our heart and deliver us.

*2 Corinthians 12:9 ESV*

*But he said to me, "My grace is sufficient for you, for my power is made perfect in weakness." Therefore, I will boast all the more gladly of my weaknesses, so that the power of Christ may rest upon me. For the sake of Christ, then, I am content with weaknesses, insults, hardships, persecutions, and calamities. For when I am weak, then I am strong.*

I've heard many people say, "God won't give us more than we can bear," but if I'm honest, I've never quite understood what that means. In reading God's word, we are assured that His grace is sufficient. This means God knows our limits and in these seasons, He will give us extraordinary strength to walk through every trial. When you feel the weakest, remember that He has strengthened us for this.

## PRAYER

God, pain is not easy and it is not something I desire. I understand the humanity of this world and I know you have prepared me for every part of it. So, when affliction comes my way, God give me wisdom on how to guard my heart. I need your grace to endure and your strength to keep going. I believe in you and I believe in your word. I know that you will heal my heart and deliver me. In Jesus' name, Amen.

# CHAPTER 6

# ARISE AND FORGIVE

*Bearing with one another and, if one has a complaint against another, forgiving each other; as the Lord has forgiven you, so you also must forgive.*

—Colossians 3:13 - (ESV)

I can't tell you how many sermons I've heard about forgiveness in my life. As a church girl, forgiveness was a popular subject to preach about so I thought I knew how to forgive. In short, say "I'm sorry" and move on. Or, if someone has wronged you, confront them, wait for them to apologize and then accept their apology. You should never say, "I'm sorry if this hurt you," because that sounds like you aren't really sorry…you're just saying it for the other person. Lastly, you can forgive but you can't forget.

There you have it! That was my 4-part forgiveness series. I had forgiveness in the bag! But then, as I began to hear my husband preach on forgiveness, I developed a completely different understanding of it. Firstly, forgiveness isn't for the one who hurt you…forgiveness is for you! When

*forgiveness isn't for the one who hurt you…forgiveness is for you!*

we refuse to forgive, the person who hurt you has control over you. The pain of their infraction stops you from producing. The offense that comes from their deeds has the power to keep you from moving forward. If you allow it to, unforgiveness will become a prison that you can't get free from. Why? Because someone else has the key to your freedom.

When you forgive, you release yourself from carrying the weight of someone else's actions. When you forgive, you allow God to remove the stones that have developed in your heart. When you forgive, you begin to walk in the same power Jesus exhibited on the cross when he said, "Father, forgive them for they know not what they do." The truth is, some people will never apologize. Some people will never acknowledge what they did to you. But you can't wait for them to say I'm sorry in order to get free. Forgiveness is an inside job.

> Every time I didn't let go of what someone said about me, or what someone did to me (directly or indirectly), I collected more baggage for the journey.

When I heard forgiveness from that perspective, it changed everything. I had never thought about it like that. I had been carrying weight in my life for a long time, and at some point, it became too heavy for me to move. Unforgiveness is baggage. Imagine walking in the airport with seven bags. How much longer would it take for you to get to your gate? How much more would it cost you to check in all of that baggage? How many flights have you missed in life all because you couldn't let it go? When we arise and forgive, we are deciding to be free from the baggage by any means necessary.

I had to forgive many people in my life, but two situations come to mind immediately. Remember, I had developed a fear of death and dying early-on in my life. It seemed as if everyone died after I got close to them. When they passed away, it was always sudden and drastic. One friend drowned in a pool. Another friend was hit by a car. But when my God-sister passed, it really took a toll on me. Because we were so close, I bonded with her on an entirely different level. Our families were so connected that most people thought we were blood sisters. She was seven years older than me, and every weekend, without fail, we'd go to her house for bible study and prayer. Her family was my family and my family was her family. During my freshman year in high school, she was just beginning college. In some ways, she was like an Elizabeth to me and I was Mary because she schooled me on what to expect at each major turning point in my life. It was a great bond. It fulfilled me in so many ways. As you know, I longed for a sister—and I think it fulfilled her too because she liked having someone she could boss around.

I'll never forget that knock on our door. Earlier that day, my God-sister had gone to work. She completed her shift and drove home as usual. We were all planning to go over to her house for bible study, but my God-sister never made it. She was minutes away from her home when a drunk driver hit her car. She did not survive the impact of the accident, and when the police came to inform her parents, they also came to our house to inform my parents. That's how close we all were. My parents were asked to come to the scene because they had to use the jaws of life to remove her from the car. I went with them but they wouldn't let me come close to the accident itself. I was too young at the time, so they made me wait across the street. I remember looking from a distance and hearing the commotion. I saw pain in everyone's eyes. I couldn't stop crying. I had so many questions. It was a horrible scene. *How would I ever forgive a drunk driver for what they did to my God-sister?* I didn't know who the driver was but he did not make it out alive either. Her life was stolen from her all because someone else decided to be mindless and inconsiderate of others.

It's one thing to hear stories about people whose families suffer loss due to a drunk driver. It's another thing to lose someone yourself. Witnessing it firsthand was almost too much to bear. For years, I remember driving close to the scene of the accident and looking away. It was so close to my home that some days, it was hard not to end up on that street. For years, I would drive the long way home to avoid it. In college, when people would drink and drive, it would infuriate me. I would lose it because my fears were triggered. During party nights, I would volunteer to be the designated driver because I didn't want anyone to go through what we went through. I thought I had forgiven the person, but I was still carrying around a lot of baggage. I had anger toward drunk drivers in general, and the guy who took her life in particular. It took me a long time to heal from it. You'll know forgiveness has taken place when resentment doesn't haunt you. One day, I remember driving down that street where the accident had taken place. By this point I was married. Before this, I would drive to the spot, look away, feel anger, and become sad. But this time, I drove past the scene and didn't feel anything. It was a small victory but I realized that I had begun to work through my unforgiveness. Finally, I felt free to let it go.

> You'll know forgiveness has taken place when you no longer feel the knots in your stomach.

As long as you do not forgive the person who hurt you, you will always remain stuck. In the beginning, I couldn't move on. I felt guilty about laughing and smiling, when my god-sister's life was taken before her time. Many times, people don't want to forgive because they feel guilty about moving on. They feel that if they forgive it will imply that they have forgotten about the person. But that is not true. If we don't forgive, then the person's death becomes a stumbling block to you. If we don't forgive, then two people die in that moment— the person we lost and the person we'll never become.

If you had passed away, would you want your family to remain stuck for the rest of their lives? Or would you want them to eventually move on and accomplish great things in your honor and memory? The enemy will plant all kinds of lies in our head to keep us from moving forward. With the drunk driver, he planted the lie that if I let go, it would be insulting to my God-sister's life. But with another situation, the enemy planted the lie that people (especially women) cannot be trusted.

My second experience with unforgiveness happened decades later. At this point, my husband and I were in full-time ministry. Our lives had completely changed. Our norm had shifted. Our friends had also changed. During that time, I met a friend—we'll call her Rita. Rita's husband was a pastor and my husband was a pastor, so we hit it off pretty quickly. Over time, our connection grew closer and closer. I found her to be open, honest, and selfless—and those were the attributes I looked for in a friend. So Rita and I became even closer. As you've learned about me, once I bring you into my inner circle, I am all-in! I became all-in with Rita and it was all good; until one day, I confided in Rita and she, in my mind, violated my trust. She shared something with someone that I didn't want to be shared. The truth is, what she did wasn't as major as I had made it. I overreacted and immediately retreated from the relationship.

Rita picked up on a major change in my behavior and one day she called me to tell me the truth: "I can't be all-in with someone who is not giving their all to the friendship." I responded, "Well I can't be all-in with someone that I can't trust." After that conversation, we ended our friendship. She went on with her life and I went on with my life. I was hurt and offended. But after I peeled back the layers of my hurt, I realized why I had overreacted.

I was triggered by what she said, and her words made me think about a past hurt that had nothing to do with her. As a girl, my trust was broken when I confided in someone very close to me, and before I could get on the bus,

> Because of my baggage, I had always been nervous about trusting women.

my secret was told and spread throughout my school. Then, in college, my trust was broken again when I confided in my college friend about a shameful secret. Before I could sit down in my next class, my secret was told to the entire campus. So, when I think about what happened with Rita and I, her mistake wasn't as serious as I had made it out to be. If 10 was the worst thing you could do, and 0 was a minor mistake, Rita's mistake was a 4. But I treated it like it was a 12! I was hypersensitive because I had never forgiven the family relative who betrayed me as a child. I also had never forgiven the college friend who betrayed me as a young adult. How many people are suffering in your present all because you have residual unforgiveness from your past? If I didn't get a handle on my baggage, I would've lost a solid friend of 8+ years.

*I am woman enough to admit when I'm wrong.*

I was wrong. I managed the relationship in a way that I shouldn't have. I was hurt but I didn't give space for a conversation or an explanation. Instead, I cut off the relationship and did not give her an opportunity to explain what was going on. Eventually, God spoke to me. The more God began to deal with my unforgiveness, the more I realized that this friendship was not one worth losing. In life, you will learn that some relationships require a necessary ending. When we are hurt beyond repair or when a friendship has become abusive, this requires a necessary ending. In this situation, I did not feel like the relationship with Rita was supposed to end. So, I reached out to her and told her some of the things I had learned from my journey. As we began to share, we both realized that we needed to offer an apology to each other. It was difficult because so much time had passed. But it was refreshing to know that our friendship could rekindle after years of silence. In the forgiveness process, it's important to talk about the things that happened in the past. When you do, it will help you to learn each other even more. I'm grateful that God gave me the strength and the courage to rekindle the relationship because it's an irreplaceable one. I'm grateful to know that God forgives us and He gives us opportunities for redemption. I'm also grateful that I learned how to give and receive forgiveness.

Since then, our friendship has been restored. Today, we are closer than we were before. We are more honest, more transparent, and I have truly forgiven her and she has forgiven me. I realize that every situation is not a "Rita situation." Depending on the health of the person, you will need to adjust accordingly. I've had to forgive some people in my life and set different boundaries to protect me from their toxicity. There are others

> Some friendships will be restored and some relationships will not. Forgiveness is not a one-size-fits-all thing.

in my life whom I've forgiven, and once we admitted our wrong and released our offense, we were able to return back to the original state of our relationship. Every situation is different. Sometimes, you need to forgive others for their mistakes, but other times you need to ask for forgiveness. Remember, hurt people hurt people. When you are hurting, it is possible for you to hurt others (consciously or unconsciously). Jesus teaches us to forgive 70 times 7. When you think about how often he forgives us, it should become easier to forgive others. Contrary to popular belief, you don't have to cut everybody off. Everyone is not your enemy. People are human and we all make mistakes. But the longer you live in unforgiveness, the longer you will suffer. The person who hurt you will have moved on and you will be stuck in a place of pain. Don't let a callous heart keep you from called life…all because you refused to RISE.

## RISE UP!

When you think about unforgiveness, there are always three areas that need to be acknowledged: God, people, and yourself. Some of us have a grudge with God. Maybe you expected God to heal your loved one. Maybe you expected God to save your marriage. When you have an offense with God, you need to ACKNOWLEDGE it. Job was distraught after he lost everything, but he acknowledged it. He told the truth even when the lie felt better. Have you ever been upset with God? Have you ever felt like God didn't live up to the expectations that you had of him? I surely wanted God to protect my friend from that drunk driver, and for a moment, I couldn't pray. I didn't know how to reconcile my anger with God's love. If you've ever been in a similar situation, remember: forgiveness takes time. Forgiveness is like peeling back an onion. Over time, you will get to the core of your real emotions but right now, you need to ACKNOWLEDGE where you are. I'm hurting. I'm angry. I'm confused. You must do the same with people who have hurt you. Consider writing a letter to the person who hurt you the most. Even if you don't give them the letter, write down your feelings. It helps to ACKNOWLEDGE where you are. Tell them why you are offended. Tell them how their decisions affected you. Write as if they will read it, but don't feel obligated to give it. Finally, when you haven't forgiven yourself, you become your worst enemy. If you've done something that you never thought you would do, give yourself permission to be human. We all make mistakes. We all fall short. If God has forgiven you, why can't you forgive yourself?

*some decisions alter relationships forever, and some mistakes are repairable.*

Again, this process requires time. So after you ACKNOWLEDGE your reality, then you need to UNCOVER the truth and replace the lie. The truth is, if I don't forgive I can't be forgiven. The truth is, broken people make poor decisions. The truth is, some decisions alter relationships forever, and some mistakes are repairable. When you UNCOVER the truth, then you can replace the lies you've told yourself. The lie I told myself was *she was wrong. This is his fault.* It was easy to cast blame on others, but I honestly had to see the bigger picture. *How did I contribute to this situation? What could I have done differently?* If I am hypersensitive, that is my issue—not theirs. If I am triggered by unresolved issues in me, that is my issue—not theirs. When I replaced the lie of my feelings with the truth of my faith, then I could EXAMINE the side-effects of unforgiveness and make a healthier choice. The side-effects are feeling stuck, unproductive, bitterness, resentment, and damaged relationships. Jesus was able to forgive Peter because Peter had a bad day. Jesus was able to walk away from Judas because Judas had a bad heart. Peter was loyal.

*As you learn to forgive others, don't confuse Peter for Judas.*

He just had a moment. Judas had a heart issue, and only God can change someone's heart. After I noticed the side-effects of unforgiveness, I had no choice but to ARISE and make the change. The first change I had to make was in me. I had to learn to be kind to others, and forgive others. I had to be willing to do to others what Christ did for me. I had to lay down my pride and apologize. I had to work toward reconciliation in some relationships, and I had to put up healthy boundaries in others. As you rise from the ashes of unforgiveness, God will give you the tools to make the right decisions. Trust that He knows what you need and He will supply every need according to his abundant grace.

# RISE UP!

1. Acknowledge: take off the blinders
2. Uncover: identify the root - replace the lie
3. Examine- evaluate the side-effects of unforgiveness
4. Arise: Make the Change

*Mark 26-11:25 ESV*

*And whenever you stand praying, forgive, if you have anything against anyone, so that your Father also who is in heaven may forgive you your trespasses."*

Forgiveness is a term that requires action. When we forgive, we release what we are carrying. But remember this: forgiveness is not for the other person, it's for you. When we withhold forgiveness from others, we are also withholding God's forgiveness towards us. I don't know about you but I refuse to let someone else stop me from receiving what God has for me. We must release them so that we can receive Him!

*Matthew 22-18:21 ESV*

*Then Peter came up and said to him, "Lord, how often will my brother sin against me, and I forgive him? As many as seven times?" Jesus said to him, "I do not say to you seven times, but seventy-seven times.*

Forgiveness is a process. At times, it will not be easy. But we must learn to keep forgiving until we no longer feel it. It's a continuous journey. My mentor, Denise Boggs, gave me the analogy of an onion one day and it helped me. Imagine peeling the onion until you got to the core (where the seed is). Forgiveness is like peeling that onion. Yes, we will shed tears and yes, we will feel pain, but we have to keep doing it until it is gone. Forgiveness is possible; you just have to stay consistent.

## PRAYER

God, you sent your son Jesus to give his life for me so that all my sins would be forgiven. You have commanded me to do the same: to forgive those who have afflicted me. I want to be obedient to your word because obedience is better than sacrifice. As of today, I have decided to release every weight that I am carrying because of someone else's action toward me. Help me to continue the process until true forgiveness has taken place. God, forgive me for not forgiving others. I release it and I'm ready to receive more of you. Amen.

CHAPTER 7

# ARISE FROM GRIEF

*I have said these things to you, that in me you may have peace. In the world, you will have tribulation. But take heart; I have overcome the world."*

–John 16:33 ESV

Two thousand, nine hundred and seventy-seven. Do you know what that number represents? Two thousand, nine hundred and seventy-seven. It is the number of people killed on 9/11. It's the number of people whose families were forever changed by one tragic event. Two thousand, nine hundred and seventy-seven funerals, phone calls, bodies to identify, and victims to bury. When you combine the passengers on all of the aircrafts, the Pentagon employees and the people who were in or around the Twin Towers on that sad day when the two buildings collapsed, the number of fatalities total at 2,977. Some families are still grieving that loss. Some people will never be the same. Even survivors are dealing with PTSD, regret and guilt because loss affects everyone.

Simply defined, grief is the sorrow one feels after a loss. Grief is a normal and natural reaction. Whenever something ends, or whenever there is a change in one's familiar pattern, grieving is necessary. But not all of us know that. Not all of us realize how important it is to grieve. Ecclesiastes 3:4 tells us that there is a time to weep and a time to laugh; a time to mourn and a time to dance. But I have witnessed so many people who have experienced loss, and instead of pausing to process their pain, they simply keep on moving. If they lose a loved one, they make funeral arrangements and go back to work the next week. If they lose their job, they apply for unemployment and immediately start searching for another job. Our pain begins to pile up in our hearts, and eventually, we explode onto others or we implode within ourselves.

*When we refuse to grieve, we refuse to heal.*

Grieving is necessary for all forms of loss. The physical loss of a loved one, the loss of a relationship, a divorce, a change in location, a change in career, the loss of control, the loss of financial stability, the loss of one's physical strength—did you know there are more than forty losses that a person can encounter in their lifetime? Many authors and psychologists help us to deal with the loss of someone we love when they die, but have you ever had to grieve something that wasn't a physical death? How do you arise from that? Can I "call out sick" if my house burns down and I lose all of my childhood memories in a fire? Will people bring food to my house if I have a miscarriage?

What about moments when everyone is celebrating a promotion or a relocation but you are sad because you will leave behind friends, memories, and rituals from your previous living arrangement?

All of my life, I wanted to have children. I remember when we were kids, we would play a game called M.A.S.H. It stood for mansion, apartment, shack, or house. During that game, we had to pick the house we would live in, the person we would marry, the car we would drive, and most importantly, the number of kids we would have. Without fail, I would always tell my friends that I wanted a boy and a girl. I loved being a mom, and I loved the idea of raising a beautiful little girl. *Fast-forward to my adult years.* God blessed my husband and I with two wonderful sons. I was so grateful for my boys, but in the back of my mind, I never let go of the idea that I would have a girl one day. It was hard news to hear but I was thankful for the two sons God blessed us with. I buried my disappointment for a while, but when I talked to my husband about it, I had to tell him the truth: my desire to have a baby girl was still there.

> Imagine how difficult it was to hear from my doctor that due to complications with both of my pregnancies, I would not be able to have more children.

Now, let me pause to explain what I believe about desires. I believe that God gives us the desires of his heart. I also believe that we should pursue those desires with all of our heart. At the same time, I think that many of us confuse His desires with our desires. We have plans, but God has a greater plan. We have a dream-life and a perfect house in mind, but God may not have that dream-life in mind for you. Jeremiah 29:11 tells us that his plans will cause us to prosper. His plans will give us hope and a future. When we walk in God's plans for us, we will prosper, we will have hope and we will have a future. If I am honest, I didn't know if it was God's plan for me to have a daughter. It may have been. All I know is that, I wanted another child and I was hoping for a girl. This desire quickly turned into determination. No matter what the obstacle was, I was going to get my little girl. So, I had another conversation with my husband and I told him what I wanted. He didn't think twice about it because he loves me and would give me the world if I asked for it. After he got on board, I began to explore different options and avenues to have a baby girl. Since I couldn't have her through natural means, I considered adoption. I considered foster care. I considered everything. When I began to research the foster care program in our local city, a woman at the church walked me through the process. She was a foster mom as well, and she answered all of my questions and introduced me to the way foster care works in New Jersey. I was fully committed to the process, and we began to fill out paperwork to become foster parents. During our initial interviews, we were very specific about what we wanted and what we didn't want. We asked for a placement that could potentially transfer from foster care into adoption. We asked for a child whose parents had relinquished their parental rights so that family members couldn't show up unexpectedly and request custody of a child who had already become attached to us. Months after we completed the preliminary process, we received the best phone call ever! A baby girl was coming home with us. The child's mother was a teenager and had decided that she didn't want to raise this child. I was so excited! My husband was a little more cautious. Naturally, he wanted to protect me and make sure I didn't experience any unnecessary hurt. He was right to do so because before we could complete the placement paperwork, we were notified that a family member called and expressed interest in the child. This angered me because I was clear about the terms of our agreement from the beginning, but the agency was not forthright with us. When we did a little more digging we discovered that this agreement was always going to be a temporary replacement. I didn't know how to respond at first, but I was definitely very sad and hurt by all of it.

> Unfortunately, after two days of living with us, the child had to leave.

I didn't want to give up that easily, so I decided to continue with the process. After a few months, we received another phone call. This was the moment I was waiting for. We were told that another child was a candidate for adoption. We agreed to meet the child, and we began to spend time with her. When she moved in with us, she was two years old and it felt like a dream come true. I had my boys, I had the love of my life, and I had the daughter that I had always wanted. As we interacted with the child, however, we began to notice things about her that didn't add up. To protect the child, I won't go into detail about our findings, but I can say that the agency wasn't honest with us about what we were going to deal with. For six months, we did everything we could to normalize the situation. But it didn't work out. Once again, we had to say goodbye to another child that we couldn't keep in our home.

Pain. All I felt was pain. I have never hurt like that before. I was devastated and distraught. I felt teased. I felt played with. It was one thing to find out that the child you prepared for couldn't stay with you. But it's another thing when the child moves into your home, spends time with your family and friends, and then, they are taken away from you without time to prepare for it. I felt like I had wanted something for so long, I was given that thing for a limited time, and then, it left me. But I knew what to do—I did what I always did: I buried my hurt. I hid my feelings and I suppressed the disappointment. To be honest, I didn't even realize I was grieving until later on when random things would happen that would trigger deep sadness. Simple things like seeing a mother pushing her daughter in a swing at the park—that triggered me. Or, hearing other members ask, "why won't you give your husband a baby girl?"—it definitely triggered me. It took me a long time to rise from this one, but as I write this book, I assure you...you can and you will rise!

*I was grieving the loss of a little girl, and I was grieving the loss of a dream that turned into a nightmare.*

## RISE UP!

*I have said these things to you, that in me you may have peace. In the world, you will have tribulation. But take heart; I have overcome the world."*

—John 16:33 ESV

Some things happen in life to grow us. I've always believed that. Pain can mature you if you let it. Mistakes can teach you a valuable lesson if you are willing to learn from them and do the work. When I experienced grief on this level, I decided to turn my obstacle into an opportunity. Who else is feeling this pain? How can I help others to find healing? I couldn't imagine how many people felt like me. I was trying my best to do my best. I loved the Lord. I loved my family. I loved my job. But I was empty. I was so sad. No scripture could pull me out of my pit (at least, not in the beginning). I couldn't even find words to describe where I was. All I knew was that I needed help. Thank God

*From the first grief class to the last, I not only found healing but I discovered my calling.*

that He loves us enough to lead us to the places that will heal us. One day, I was introduced to the Grief Recovery Institute. This support group was created to walk alongside people who experienced loss. God allowed me to experience this "affliction" so that he could reveal his next "assignment." Before I knew it, the scales were removed from my eyes. This was the peace that he promised in John 16:33. My peace wasn't that God would give me what I wanted. My peace wasn't that I would never suffer. Jesus told us that we would have tribulation in this world. I'm so glad he told us what to expect, otherwise I would've thought I was doing something wrong. But in the midst of the tribulation, he promised that we would overcome. Once I began to heal, I decided to go back to the Grief Recovery Institute to complete my certification. In October of 2015, I completed the coursework, obtained my certificate and became a certified grief recovery specialist. My pain pushed me to purpose. My obstacle became an opportunity. Today, I help my husband to minister to the unspoken wounds, unmet needs, and devastating losses that affect members in our church. We have designed curriculums, classes, intensives, and resources to help others to face their grief. When I think about everything I lost in my life, and all of the tears I cried, I realized that God kept his promises! He used all of it for my good.

Like everything else, my turnaround began when I acknowledged what I was really feeling. I had to ACKNOWLEDGE the void. I had to ACKNOWLEDGE the shame. I had to ACKNOWLEDGE the fact that I didn't want to face the world. I didn't want to hear their questions—what happened? Where is she? How is she? Some days I just wanted to lay in my bed and cry. My next step was to UNCOVER the wounds and identify the root. The root of my grief was unprocessed pain. I had never really processed any of the losses before this one, so when I experienced this, it was worse than ever! Even after the second child left our home, I still didn't know how to handle my grief. So, I tried to replace her presence with something else. Many people who grieve do the same thing—in order to avoid the hurt, they look for a temporary replacement. The replacement becomes anesthesia for their wounds, but it doesn't fix their problems. My temporary fix was a dog. I figured if I could buy a dog then I could distract myself from the hurt. But it didn't work. I had no emotional connection to our dog. I couldn't get excited about our dog. I bought the dog clothes. I attempted to dress up the dog. I took the dog out for walks in the park—I did everything! But I felt nothing. Eventually, I had to give our dog away because I wasn't ready to embrace something new until I had processed the old. Sometimes, you've got to stop and just feel the pain. Don't go on a date just

*Don't rush to toxic habits and addictions—stop and feel the pain.*

yet—stop and feel the pain. When I stopped to feel it, God began to fix it. In the uncovering, God started to minister to each hurt one by one.

As I uncovered the wounds of my disappointment, I also replaced the lie with the truth. Some lies I had learned in church, but they weren't true—*God needed her more. Don't cry about it…shout about it. Get up and work through it. Find something to replace it with immediately.* The church clichés weren't helping me.

When I read the Word, I learned the truth. I wouldn't weep forever. Joy was going to come. I saw how Jesus took time to weep after he lost Lazarus. It encouraged me to pause and weep as well. When I saw the heartbreak of Christ on the cross when he felt forsaken, it all helped me to reconcile my feelings and emotions. This allowed me to EXAMINE the side-effects—anger, anxiety, attitude shifts, confrontation, depression and impatience—how could I minister to others if these side-effects remained within me? I had to make a change and RISE. The second thing that helped me to make a change, after connecting with the grief support group, was the Word of God. I needed to deepen my devotional time. I had to find other women who experienced grief just like me. Do you know

*how could I minister to others if these side-effects remained within me? I had to make a change and rise.*

how many women in the Bible dealt with grief? Think about Hannah. She was barren and couldn't have children. She grew up dealing with the loss of purpose. She felt as if she had no calling if she didn't have a child. But God used her barrenness to bless others. Sarah was too old. She was so old that she laughed when she was told she would have a child. And even after she had him, her husband had to wrestle with losing him. Sure, God spared Isaac's life but I'm sure Abraham and Sarah can relate to the pain we feel when it seems like God is saying one thing and doing another. Naomi had lost her husband and her sons. At that time, the men in her life were responsible for providing for her in every way. She not only lost the loves of her life but she also lost her provision. Mary, the mother of Jesus, had to grieve the loss of her son on a cross. To everyone else, he was Jesus Christ. But to her, he was her baby. When Jesus died, she had to grieve even though his death brought us life. Above the loss of life, or the loss of a relationship, I want you to know that God can give you the power to rise from this. You won't be able to do this alone. I encourage you to search out recovery groups or counselors that can help you discern next steps. If you are reading this, there is still hope. You can recover from this, and God will be with you every step of the way.

# RISE UP!

1. Acknowledge: take off the blinders

2. Uncover: identify the root - replace the lie

3. Examine- evaluate the side-effects of grief

4. Arise: Make the Change

## SCRIPTURES

*Ecclesiastes 8-3:1 ESV*

*For everything there is a season, and a time for every matter under heaven: a time to be born, and a time to die; a time to plant, and a time to pluck up what is planted; a time to kill, and a time to heal; a time to break down, and a time to build up; a time to weep, and a time to laugh; a time to mourn, and a time to dance; a time to cast away stones, and a time to gather stones together; a time to embrace, and a time to refrain from embracing; a time to seek, and a time to lose; a time to keep, and a time to cast away; a time to tear, and a time to sew; a time to keep silence, and a time to speak; a time to love, and a time to hate; a time for war, and a time for peace.*

Grief is normal and necessary. There are many losses that we will encounter in life. When we are filled with grief, we have to allow the process to be the process. Loss causes us to have questions and it can also cause us to not want to deal with it. Grief doesn't go away with time—it has to be worked through. Because seasons come and seasons go, make sure that you don't carry old seasons into new seasons. Grieving doesn't mean we will forget what we have lost but it does mean we will find a completion and healing during the process.

## PRAYER

God...the loss is unbearable but I understand that there is a season for everything. I am comforted that you will be here with me in my time of loss. Thank you for allowing me to feel what I feel. God, I need peace in this. I don't understand why this has happened but I trust you. I need your strength and your comfort to endure this season. I look to you for my help and I will walk through this season without residue. Amen.

# CHAPTER 8

# ARISE FROM OVER-FUNCTIONING

*And she had a sister called Mary, who sat at the Lord's feet and listened to his teaching. But Martha was distracted with much serving. And she went up to him and said, "Lord, do you not care that my sister has left me to serve alone? Tell her then to help me." But the Lord answered her, "Martha, Martha, you are anxious and troubled about many things, but one thing is necessary. Mary has chosen the good portion, which will not be taken away from her."*

–Luke 10:39- 42

Applying for a job is nerve-wracking. In order to do well, you have to "look the part," arrive on time, and research the company thoroughly. The interview process is a major factor. One wrong answer could eliminate you from consideration. The question that usually trips people up is "What are your strengths and weaknesses?" Over time, people have changed their response to that question. When I was in college, most interviewees would say, "my strength is that I'm a perfectionist." We said this because we wanted our future employer to know we were committed to seeing a task through until it was perfect. But nowadays, a lot of people see perfectionism as a weakness. We have started to embrace our limitations, and now more than ever before, we are learning that perfectionism is an unrealistic goal.

Growing up, I struggled with perfectionism, too. Failure wasn't an option so I needed to get an A on every test. I needed to help every friend with their homework, remove every spot off of the bathroom floor, dot every I and cross every T. Even when I got married, I put my family through torture for years! I created a list of rules for my husband after we said, "I do." He couldn't sit on certain furniture, he had to pull the bedroom covers back a certain way before he got into the bed—no shoes on the carpet, no this, no that—do this, do that! You would've thought our home was a military base! I didn't see how stressful I had become and how uncomfortable he had become. Suffice it to say, this arrangement didn't last very long, but I thought it was perfectionism. In actuality, I was struggling with over-functioning. I was introduced to this term when I read *Emotionally Healthy Woman* by Geri Scazzero. The moment I read the definition, the scales were removed from my eyes.

In the opening chapter, Geri writes:

*We overfunction when we do for others what they can and should do for themselves. Overfunctioners prevent people, including themselves, from growing up. The*

*street, however, runs both ways. Wherever you find an overfunctioner, an under-functioner inevitably follows close behind. Overfunctioning dangerously imperils friendships, marriages, churches, workplaces, and families. I know this well. I was an overfunctioner for many years....*
*Let me repeat: Overfunctioning is doing for others what they can and should do for themselves. Overfunctioning is more than simply a bad habit; it is a weed whose deep roots can often be traced back through generations in your family of origin. And the thorny branches of that weed reach far out into our workplaces, parenting, marriages, churches, and friendships.*

Wow! This definition floors me every time I read it. Immediately after reading Scazzero's words, I thought about Mary and Martha in the Bible. Mary was the sister who had an amazing devotional life. She was devoted to God and committed to prayer. She enjoyed worshipping at the feet of Jesus. But Martha was the sister who had to deal with every-day life. Modern-day Martha's are mothers, wives, and CEOs. Martha has a lot of responsibility, but something is missing from her life. She is working hard but Martha is in desperate need of a Sabbath. Martha is the woman who needs to just stop, take time to reflect on who she is, and spend time with God. I empathize with Martha. I can relate to her struggle. As a wife, mother, boss, and friend, I know what it's like to get caught in the world of to-do lists and endless tasks. At one point in my life, I would make to do lists and if I didn't get everything done that was on my list, I would feel as if I failed for the day. Imagine how Martha felt when Jesus came over and the food wasn't ready?!? Martha, like me, was an over-functioner.

For a long time, I didn't see anything wrong with over-functioning. In fact, I applauded myself and others awarded me because of it. Everybody used to call me "Superwoman" because I literally did everything for everyone. I took care of the laundry at home. I cooked three different meals at night for my family because each person had different allergies. I helped the kids with homework. I drove their friends to practice. I showed up to PTA meetings. I made sure to serve my husband and fulfill my role. At work, I was the administrator, the problem-solver, the analyzer and the counselor. To me, this was success. This was what every woman needed to be. My strength was in my perfectionism, or said better, in my over-functioning! But in real time, I was exhausted.

Have you ever turned a weakness into a strength? Can you relate to Martha and I? Like Martha, something was missing from my life. I had a relationship with God, but if I am honest, I always tried to fit God in. On the one hand, I knew that without him I could do nothing. The problem was, I was trying to fit him in instead of making him first. At that time, I gave God "on the run" prayers. I listened to worship in my car on the way to school or work. I did a quick 5-minute devotional while cooking breakfast. None of this was bad, but something was still missing. I needed to be still in God's presence. I needed to give Him my undivided attention. I knew that I needed to make adjustments but I didn't know how. It got so bad that I didn't want anyone doing anything in our home. If they tried to, I would get offended. My over-functioning met a need that I had to be useful. I needed people to value me, so I lived out of need instead of calling. I was affirmed when others needed me. So, when my children were younger, they had weekly chores and tasks to do around the house. If I told them to have their rooms spotless by Wednesday at 8pm, on Tuesday by 12noon, I would go in their room and clean it up before they got home from school. I wanted them to come back and say, "Wow I have a great mom. She does everything for me." That was a consequence of my over-functioning. When my husband tried to delegate others to help me with some of my workload, I became irritable and offended. He was only trying to relieve me and help me but I felt like he was implying that I wasn't able to maintain everything on my own.

I began to see my problem as a real issue when my youngest son did something that rocked my world. Seth and Gabe have opposite personalities. My oldest, Seth, is nonchalant and calm. He goes with the flow. He is also my side-kick. He eats what I eat when I cook, he'll ride to the mall with me, and he will compliment my new hairstyle or notice small details about the littlest things. My baby, Gabe, on the other hand is a totally different blessing. He requires a special love language, and many times, I'd serve him like he was second husband!

One night, after cooking separate meals for Dharius, Gabe, and Seth, I called the boys down and told them that dinner was ready. Seth came down, fixed his plate, and finished his food in minutes. A few minutes passed, and I noticed that Gabriel hadn't come down to the kitchen to make his plate. I called him again and told him to come eat. He responded, "I will sit down when my plate is on the table."

*BOOM!*

Can you imagine how wide my eyes opened? Now, of course, I know my son—and if you know anything about Gabe, he is the sarcastic comedian in our family. I knew he wasn't being disrespectful, but his words opened my eyes in a major way. I was doing too much. My children were not learning to be responsible. They were depending on me to save them, clean their room, and fix their plate. Whether I wanted to or not, it was time for me to rise...and that's exactly what I did!

## RISE UP!

*And she had a sister called Mary, who sat at the Lord's feet and listened to his teaching. But Martha was distracted with much serving. And she went up to him and said, "Lord, do you not care that my sister has left me to serve alone? Tell her then to help me." But the Lord answered her, "Martha, Martha, you are anxious and troubled about many things, but one thing is necessary. Mary has chosen the good portion, which will not be taken away from her."*

–Luke 10:39- 42

When I decided to rise in the area of over-functioning, let me tell you the blunt truth—the transition was not easy. Whenever you make a decision to stop doing for others what they can do for themselves, "others" will not be happy. They were just fine with things as they were. Your boss was just fine with you coming in early and leaving late. Your friends were just fine with you babysitting their kids without pay. The neighbors were just fine with you shoveling their snow and mowing their lawn. Your children were just fine with things the way they were. But I needed to make the change for myself and for my boys. If I didn't correct it, in 15 years, they would be searching for a robot as a wife and not a woman! They would expect a maid and not a mate. I couldn't do that to them. They needed to adjust their expectations quickly.

Of course, I still spoil my children, but now, we function as a healthy household. Everyone has responsibilities and they do their part. At work, the same thing had to happen. I could no longer rescue people from their responsibilities. I had to stand back and let someone fall, even if I saw it failing. Otherwise, they would've never learned how to pick it back up and fix it without me. My

"ACKNOWLEDGEMENT MOMENT" happened at the dinner table, but it showed up in every area of my life. I was neglecting my most important relationship—God—and not setting boundaries in my secondary relationships. After I acknowledged that my priorities were misplaced, I then began to UNCOVER the origin of my problem. The root cause of my over-functioning was something that ran through my blood. All of the women in my family were over-functioners. They were resilient. They were go-getters. My mom was a strong woman. She had her first child at an early age. She raised her children on her own. She went back to college as a mother of two. She paid her way through school while raising two boys so she could better herself and have a successful career. I marinated in the womb of an over-functioner. The positive side was that I had a strong work ethic. But the negative side was that I became anxious when I wasn't in control.

When I UNCOVERED the root, I was able to replace the lie with the truth. The lies were "grind today, rest when you die," or "if you don't do it, nobody else will." The truth is, I am not a robot. I am fearfully and wonderfully made. I am not supposed to save others. Jesus is our savior. The other truth that I didn't really see until now was this—I was already enough. I was doing things for others to receive affirmation, but in God's eyes (and in the eyes of those who loved me) I was already enough. I was already loved, appreciated, accepted, and affirmed. My works didn't make my husband love me more. My meals didn't make my children appreciate me any more than they already had. I was enough.

Once I replaced the lie with the truth, I had to EXAMINE the side-effects of over-functioning. If I continued to live the way I was living, I would not be around to enjoy my children grow up. I would never stop working even when I was on vacation. Most of all, my relationship with God would always come last but not least. Realizing this helped me to ARISE and make the change. I began my change by focusing my energy on the essentials. I organized my life around my priorities, and I didn't allow my time to tell me what to do. I had to manage my work life and my home life better. In short, I had to simplify. In your life, what can be simplified? How are you over-functioning? I encourage you to list your non-negotiables, your optional roles and responsibilities and adjust accordingly.

# RISE UP!

1. Acknowledge: take off the blinders
2. Uncover: identify the root - replace the lie.
3. Examine: evaluate the side-effects of Overfunctioning.
4. Arise: Make the Change

*Psalm 9-52:8 ESV*

*But I am like a green olive tree in the house of God. I trust in the steadfast love of God forever and ever. I will thank you forever, because you have done it. I will wait for your name, for it is good, in the presence of the godly.*

Over-functioning can cause a person to focus on everything and everyone else so much, that they forget about themselves. We need to get planted in God so that we can grow and be nurtured by Him. We have to release the need for control and trust God. As we are planted in God, we will receive the fruit from our labor. We can lean on Him, confide in Him, and depend on Him. He is there nurturing us when no one else is.

*Galatians 23-5:22 ESV*

*But the fruit of the Spirit is love, joy, peace, patience, kindness, goodness, faithfulness, gentleness, self-control; against such things there is no law.*

When we over-function we are searching for approval, affirmation, validation and more. But remember, God is the true source of everything we need. At times, it is easy to slip back into over-functioning because it is our default. We have to practice discipline and self-control to keep from sliding back.

## PRAYER

God, I realize that you are the only that can fill every void. I have allowed what I do to validate me and to fill my empty places. Help me today to be disciplined enough to say no when necessary. You are the only one who gives me patience and self-control. Help me to be patient with myself when I have not met my expectations. Whenever I am searching for approval, affirmation or attention, help me to use wisdom on how to receive them in a healthy way. Amen

# CHAPTER 9

# ARISE AND ROAR

*Arise, shine, for your light has come, and the glory of the LORD has risen upon you.*

The journey has not been easy. Some days have been harder than others. The people who start with you will not always end with you. But in the end, you can arise. You can arise out of whatever you are going through. You can arise from the negativity you've heard and believed. You can arise from the trauma of yesterday. You can arise! Whether you've experienced rejection, insecurity, fear, conditional love, grief, unforgiveness, or over-functioning, nothing will stop you when you determine to rise.

Around the time that I was writing this book, I was also preparing for my women's conference. Two or three times a year, I try to plan something unique for the women of Change Church so we can connect with the vision of our church, and so I can love on the ladies a little bit. As I was preparing for the conference, I began to do research on lionesses. I was amazed by some of the information I discovered. First of all, a lioness is known for her hunt. Did you know that the female lion, not the male lion, is primarily responsible for hunting for her family? Her hunt usually occurs after dark, and because a lioness is the primary caregiver for her cubs, she won't stop until she finds something that will sustain her household. In the same way, we are called to rise to the occasion and care for all that God has entrusted to us. You may be more focused at night or in the morning, but every person needs a time of pursue and a time to hunt. When we finally lay aside the weights we have discussed previously, we can fully be who God called us to be.

In addition, lionesses are known for their eyesight and vision. It would make sense that lionesses would need outstanding vision if they are hunting at night. During the night, they are looking for hidden jewels in dark places to sustain their family. Likewise, when we rise from our pain, God will give us vision for our purpose. God has blessed you with vision and insight to see what others cannot see. God has increased your sensitivity to discern what others would misunderstand.

Don't forsake your greatest weapon. You have been blessed to see in the dark, to recognize what others ignore, and to conquer despite every obstacle.

When I think about my life, especially in connection to my husband, I can honestly say that he has helped me to see things about myself that I needed to see; and I have helped him to do the same. I cover his blindspots. I look where no one is looking. I try my best to cover my children by seeing a problem before the problem ever shows up. God wants to use you to do the same thing for your family. When you finally recognize your strength, the enemy will get nervous and hide. But a lioness will find its enemy and conquer. Why? Because a lioness is known for her fight and for her roar. She is resilient. She is determined. She doesn't back down easily. Her bark and her bite are serious! Her roar tells others that "Momma is here." Her roar is a signal that help has arrived.

God has given you the power to combat serpents and scorpions. God has equipped you with everything you need to have the victory. Your fight is not like others. Your fight is a spiritual one. So, put on the whole armor of God and fight! This was the second scripture my mother taught

*When you begin to rise from the lies of your past, you will uncover the truth of your power.*

me growing up, and I am so grateful she planted that seed in me. Every morning, I would quote Ephesians 6:11 – Put on God's whole armor [the armor of a heavy-armed soldier which God supplies], that you may be able to successfully stand up against [all] the strategies and the deceits of the devil. Remember, to be saved is not to be passive. Every now and then, you must fight back. Every now and then, you must allow God to stand up in you and reclaim your family, reclaim your focus, and reclaim your purpose. God has deposited too much in you for you to remain silent. Let your roar signal to others that "God is here." Let your roar remind your past that you don't belong there anymore. Your roars tells the enemy that settling is not an option. Don't allow anything to stop you from the abundant life God promised you.

When I think about my life in comparison to this lioness, I am encouraged to know that God will supply all of my needs. He will give me what I need even when He doesn't give it to me when I want it. One thing that every lioness needs is a pack of trusted lions and lionesses around her. In my world, I needed a circle of life-giving agents who would speak life into me. I am grateful that God brought specific people into my life who played a significant role in my metamorphosis. I know for sure that I wouldn't have been able to arise without their help. As I begin to list my life-giving agents, I want you to think about who is giving life to you. Who is helping you to rise? Who is distracting you from rising? Once you identify those two groups, make room for God to send you what you need in the right time and season.

First of all, my husband. Dharius Daniels has been the consistency in my life. I respect him for loving me in my brokenness and walking with me through my journey to wholeness. I can't imagine what it must have been like to deal with me in my dysfunctional state. I always tried to honor and serve my husband, but I didn't always know how to love him the way he needed to be loved. Nevertheless, he's been so patient with me. He has prayed for me and he has encouraged me even when I wanted to walk away from it all.

A few years ago, I was so confused and lonely. I was "in my feelings" and I was tired of pretending that everything was OK. For years, my husband would tell me that I was like a bucket with holes. The more he poured into me, the more his love would leak out. I never understood what he meant, but God knew what do to. He brought Dr. RA Vernon and Lady Victory Vernon into our lives. We went to dinner with them one night, and within five minutes of our conversation, Dr. Vernon began to see behind my mask. He called me out like no one else had ever done. He saw my broken places and spoke to it directly. I had been wearing a mask for so long that I didn't even know it was on. I had convinced myself that everything was great, but it wasn't—and it was affecting everyone around me. Dr. Vernon and Lady Vernon helped me to tear down the walls of my shame. I started building that wall at 13 years old when a traumatic experience left me feeling stuck. I continued to pile on more baggage as life continued, and the side-effects of carrying overweight issues began to

*I was trying to do what God called me to do, but I didn't know that your calling is not your healing.*

weigh on me. I didn't know that you can be called by God and still hurting because of others. I honestly thought that as a pastor's wife, I would heal myself as I helped others to heal. But after Dr. Vernon helped me to take the blinders off, I knew I had to make a permanent change.

Around that same time, God brought Denise Boggs into my life. We met at a conference and she handed me a brochure about her retreat center. I smiled politely and went on with my day. At that time, I wasn't ready to tap into my brokenness, but when I was ready to do the work, I contacted her, and God literally used Denise Boggs to change my life. She helped to save me, she helped to save my marriage, and she helped me to rediscover my purpose. She taught me how to identify the root, examine the side-effects, and grieve the losses. Because of her, I found healing and wholeness. I learned to truly forgive those who hurt me, and I learned to let it go for real. This was not easy. It took a lot of time. But through commitment, consistency, and encouragement, I was able to take the tools she gave me and help others to heal as well.

I don't know who your coaches are. I don't know who your life-giving agents are. But I am sure that God will bring people into your life to help you shift from brokenness to wholeness. Healing is a process. You will weep some nights.

You will feel as if you just want to quit. You may be feeling empty right now. I felt all of those things and I did not know what to do next. But I decided to put one foot in front of the other, and work the little faith I

*If brokenness does not happen overnight, then neither will healing.*

had that day. Over time, I learned who Shameka was. I learned to embrace my feelings and manage them well. I exposed myself to life-giving resources and relationships that kept me accountable whenever I wanted to slide back into old patterns and behaviors. Lysa Terkuerst's devotional helped me to understand that "feelings are indicators, not dictators." Those words unglued me forever. I used to see my feelings as reactionary and unnecessary, but once the lightbulb went off for me, everything began to change. I learned how to be a better parent. I learned how to be a better child. I didn't realize how my lack of presence in both my children's lives and my parent's lives affected them. I was physically present at everything, but I was mentally and emotionally absent. I had to learn how to leave "the world of work" and step into the world of my boys. Once I did that, our relationship changed. I began to mother them more intentionally. I also became a better wife. I studied my husband's emotional needs and I stopped trying to "fix him." Once we learned more about each other—without filters or fakeness—our communication improved. Today, our love for one another is unexplainable. I not only have a husband to love, but I have a best friend with whom I can be naked and unashamed. I stopped seeing my husband as the criticizer, and I began to embrace him for who he always tried to be: my encourager and supporter. Finally, I learned how to be a better friend. I used to see relationships as transactional but as I healed from old baggage and defense mechanisms, I began to evaluate my circles. Through that, I learned how to love again. I realized that friendships are valuable assets, and in order to have a friend, you must show yourself friendly. I practiced being more present, more transparent, and more encouraging.

You never know how your brokenness will show up in a room. I didn't even realize that I was hurting the people who were closest to me. I just thought I was protecting myself from more pain. But thank God for truthful friends. It was a close friend, Michelle Aranza, who told me that when she first met me, I was cold and detached.

*when God sends you true friends, they see beyond the person you're pretending to be.*

I didn't engage her in conversation and my demeanor was disconnected. Wow! I thought I had done a pretty good job covering that up, but when God sends you true friends, they see beyond the person you're pretending to be.

Presently, Michelle and I talk with honesty, openness, and candor. Her experience of me now is that I am a "new Shameka." Only God's healing can renew your joy and give you peace. I thank God that He has blessed me with two great friends—Jacob Aranza and Michelle Aranza. He and his wife Michelle were instrumental in my "rising revelations." We grew closer and closer as the years went by, and one day Michelle took a chance on me and invited me to come to her "Arise" conference. She asked me to speak to women regarding wholeness and healing. Her invitation unlocked something in me that I didn't know was there. I was honored to do it, but I had never spoken to a crowd that large. Trust me, I second-guessed the invitation because I was still adjusting to the new Shameka. But after I replaced the lies of the enemy with the truth of God's word, I agreed to attend and that conference was a launching pad for me. I began to fight back and roar. As I prayed about what to share, God spoke to me and gave me precisely what I needed to say. Unlike other times, I didn't read multiple books and google other sources endlessly. This time, I just sat down and began to type from my heart. When I arrived at the conference, one of my favorite authors was speaking. She was so eloquent, charismatic, and moving. One the one hand, I was happy to receive. On the other hand, the "old Shameka" would've packed her bags and left the conference early. The old Shameka would've felt intimidated and "not enough." *How will I measure up to this author? I'm not as good as her.* But the new Shameka decided to arise. The peace of God came over me, and I became content and present. I enjoyed her message, and I gave my message. I didn't compare myself or change my notes. I spoke what God told me to say and after I spoke, something shifted in my life. God had used the Arise conference as a place of rebirth. It was there that I developed the courage to tell my story with the world.

I share my journey with you because I want you to know that healing is possible for you, too. During moments of rejection, insecurity, fear, grief, unforgiveness, over-functioning, and hurt, remember who you are in God. When something or someone tries to pull you backward, speak these affirmations over yourself. As you do so, God will exchange the weight of your brokenness with the beauty of his wholeness.

# RISE UP!

## I AM LOVED

*God loves me unconditionally*

*John 3:16 - For God so loved the world that he gave his one and only Son, that whoever believes in him shall not perish but have eternal life.*

*Matthew 3:17 - and behold, a voice from heaven said,*

*"This is my beloved Son,[a] with whom I am well pleased."*

### Write your own affirmation about
### God's love below

_____

_____

_____

_____

_____

_____

_____

_____

_____

_____

_____

# RISE UP!

## I AM CONFIDENT AND WORTHY

*God has supplied everything I need to succeed*

*2 Timothy 1:7. For God did not give us a spirit of timidity (of cowardice, of craven and cringing and fawning fear), but He has given us a spirit of power and of love and of calm and well-balanced mind and discipline and self-control.*

*Hebrews 4:16 Let us then fearlessly and confidently and boldly draw near to the throne of grace (the throne of God's unmerited favor to us sinners), that we may receive mercy for our failures and find grace to help in good time for every need appropriate help and well-timed help, coming just when we need it.*

*2 Corinthians 12:9 ESV. But he said to me, "My grace is sufficient for you, for my power is made perfect in weakness." Therefore I will boast all the more gladly of my weaknesses, so that the power of Christ may rest upon me.*

### Write your own affirmation about being confident and worthy in God

_____

_____

_____

_____

_____

_____

# RISE UP!
## I AM SECURE AND SAFE

*God is my shield. I am safe in his arms.*

*Isaiah 41:10 Fear not there is nothing to fear, for I am with you; do not look around you in terror and be dismayed, for I am your God. I will strengthen and harden you to difficulties, yes, I will help you; yes, I will hold you up and retain you with My victorious right hand of rightness and justice.*

*2 Thessalonians 3:3 Yet the Lord is faithful, and He will strengthen you and set you on a firm foundation and guard you from the evil one.*

*Psalm 46:1 GOD IS our Refuge and Strength mighty and impenetrable to temptation, a very present and well-proved help in trouble.*

*1 Corinthians 10:13 For no temptation (no trial regarded as enticing to sin), no matter how it comes or where it leads has overtaken you and laid hold on you that is not common to man that is, no temptation or trial has come to you that is beyond human resistance and that is not adjusted and adapted and belonging to human experience, and such as man can bear. But God is faithful to His Word and to His compassionate nature, and He can be trusted not to let you be tempted and tried and assayed beyond your ability and strength of resistance and power to endure, but with the temptation He will always also provide the way out (the means of escape to a landing place), that you may be capable and strong and powerful to bear up under it patiently.*

## Write your own affirmation about being secure and safe in God

_____

_____

_____

_____

_____

_____

_____

_____

_____

_____

_____

_____

_____

_____

_____

_____

_____

# RISE UP!

## I AM WISE

*God has given me wisdom for every circumstance.*

*Matthew 10:16 - "Behold, I am sending you out as sheep in the midst of wolves, so be wise as serpents and innocent as doves.*

*Proverbs 9:10 The fear of the Lord is the beginning of wisdom and the knowledge of the Holy One is understanding.*

## Write your own affirmation about
## God's wisdom below

_____

_____

_____

_____

_____

_____

_____

_____

_____

_____

_____

# RISE UP!

## I AM NOT ALONE

*God is with me. He will never leave me*

*Deuteronomy 31:6 Be strong and courageous. Do not be afraid or terrified because of them, for the Lord your God goes with you; he will never leave you nor forsake you."*

*Matthew 28:20 …And behold, I am with you always, to the end of the age."*

*Psalm 23:4 Even though I walk through the darkest valley, I will fear no evil, for you are with me; your rod and your staff, they comfort me.*

## Write your own affirmation about God's promise to be with you

_____

_____

_____

_____

_____

_____

_____

_____

_____

# RISE UP!

## I AM HEALED

*By His stripes, I am healed—emotionally, physically, and relationally.*

*Isaiah 53:5 But He was wounded for our transgressions,*
*He was bruised for our iniquities;*
*The chastisement for our peace was upon Him,*
*And by His stripes we are healed.*

*Psalm 103:3 He continues to forgive all your sins, he continues to heal all your diseases*

### Write your own affirmation about healing below

_____

_____

_____

_____

_____

_____

_____

_____

_____

# RISE UP!

## I WILL RISE

*God has made me more than a conqueror*

*Romans 39-8:31 - What, then, shall we say in response to these things? If God is for us, who can be against us? He who did not spare his own Son, but gave him up for us all—how will he not also, along with him, graciously give us all things? Who will bring any charge against those whom God has chosen? It is God who justifies. Who then is the one who condemns? No one. Christ Jesus who died—more than that, who was raised to life—is at the right hand of God and is also interceding for us. Who shall separate us from the love of Christ? Shall trouble or hardship or persecution or famine or nakedness or danger or sword? As it is written: "For your sake we face death all day long; we are considered as sheep to be slaughtered."[a] No, in all these things we are more than conquerors through him who loved us. For I am convinced that neither death nor life, neither angels nor demons,[b] neither the present nor the future, nor any powers, neither height nor depth, nor anything else in all creation, will be able to separate us from the love of God that is in Christ Jesus our Lord.*

Write your own affirmation about rising to be
who God called you to be

_____

_____

_____

_____

_____

_____

_____

_____

_____

_____

_____

_____

_____

_____

_____

_____

_____

_____

# RISE UP!

## I WILL ROAR

*God will help me to speak the truth in love.*

*Hebrews 4:16 So let us keep on coming boldly to the throne of grace, so that we may obtain mercy and find grace to help us in our time of need.*

*2 Timothy 4:2 I can't impress this on you too strongly. God is looking over your shoulder. Christ himself is the Judge, with the final say on everyone, living and dead. He is about to break into the open with his rule, so proclaim the Message with intensity; keep on your watch. Challenge, warn, and urge your people. Don't ever quit. Just keep it simple.*

*1 Corinthians 15:58 - Therefore, my dear brothers and sisters, stand firm. Let nothing move you. Always give yourselves fully to the work of the Lord, because you know that your labor in the Lord is not in vain.*

**Write your own affirmation about roaring until you fully walk into your purpose**

_____

_____

_____

_____

_____

_____

_____

# RISE UP!

## I WILL FIGHT AND NOT GIVE UP

*When I am weak, God is strong.*

*2 Corinthians 12:10 For the sake of Christ, then, I am content with weaknesses, insults, hardships, persecutions, and calamities. For when I am weak, then I am strong.*

*Ephesians 6:10 - Finally, be strong in the Lord and in his mighty power.*

*Isaiah 54:4 "Do not be afraid; you will not be put to shame. Do not fear disgrace; you will not be humiliated. You will forget the shame of your youth and remember no more the reproach of your widowhood.*

*John 14:27 Peace I leave with you; my peace I give you. I do not give to you as the world gives. Do not let your hearts be troubled and do not be afraid.*

## Write your own affirmation about perseveringthrough difficulty

_____

_____

_____

_____

_____